P. 45
Diversity of Home

P. 2 Definition
Household

D1466693

PRAISE FOR
Christian Households

Faced with new and contentious questions about human relationships that are bodily, and therefore physical, Breidenthal is not content with the surface rearrangements that so often pass for moral theology. His book is radical—it goes to the roots—in its examination of the deepest norms of Christian life together. Beginning with the great commandment of loving one's neighbor, Breidenthal unfolds its meaning as he works towards the concrete practices which promote that participation in the body of Christ which is Christian householding. The result of this approach is a book that grows like a tree from roots that are at once biblically and philosophically solid toward branches that bear fruit in sound practical principles. Breidenthal's innovative and challenging conclusions stand squarely within the great tradition of Christian moral theology.

—*Charles Hefling,*
Boston College

Professor Breidenthal offers us a profoundly biblical approach to the birth-created and covenanted living arrangements that Christians enter into with one another. While the author's conclusions on same-sex households remain controversial, most readers will acknowledge that he makes every effort to treat the relevant New Testament texts in a fair-minded manner.

—*John Koenig,*
The General Theological Seminary

Christian Households

CHRISTIAN HOUSEHOLDS

The Sanctification of Nearness

Thomas E. Breidenthal

Wipf & Stock
PUBLISHERS
Eugene, Oregon

Wipf and Stock Publishers
199 W 8th Ave, Suite 3
Eugene, OR 97401

Christian Households
The Sanctification of Nearness
By Breidenthal, Thomas E.
Copyright©1997 by Breidenthal, Thomas E.
ISBN: 1-59244-886-0
Publication date 9/27/2004
Previously published by Cowley Publications, 1997

To Margaret, Magdalene, and Lucy

Contents

Acknowledgments

This book emerges from my life with my wife and daughters, and from the wonderful particularities of work and residence at The General Theological Seminary—a varied collection of Christian households if ever there was one. Whatever sound moral theology may be found here is owing to the influence of my teachers, James McClendon and Oliver O'Donovan. Whatever clarity of thought and expression may be found here is owing to the patience of my students in a course entitled *The Christian Household*, taught in the Easter term of 1995: Peter Grandell, Carol Horton, Steven Woolley, Ann Matsumoto, and Lynn Ramshaw.

The physical presence of other Christians is a source of incomparable joy and strength to the believer....Each human being is created a body, the Son of God appeared on earth in the body, he was raised in the body, in the Sacrament the believer receives the Lord Christ in the body and the resurrection of the dead will bring about the perfected fellowship of God's spiritual-physical creatures....

How inexhaustible are the riches that open up for those who by God's will are privileged to live in the daily fellowship of life with other Christians!

—from Life Together *by Dietrich Bonhoeffer*

Chapter One

Why Live Together?

Why do Christians live together in the first place? Dietrich Bonhoeffer addressed this question in a small book entitled *Life Together*, written in 1938 for his friends and students in the Confessing Church. His answer is unequivocal: "The believer feels no shame, as though he were still living too much in the flesh, when he yearns for the physical presence of other Christians."[1] Bonhoeffer goes on to remind his readers that there are many kinds of Christian community. He singles out as special blessings "the privilege of living a Christian life in the fellowship of one's family," and "the gift of common life" which seminarians enjoy "for a definite period" before their ordination.

Bonhoeffer's discussion draws attention to the concreteness and physicality of life together, and to the variety of forms which Christian householding, like all householding, can take. Bonhoeffer specifically mentions families (presumably he has the nuclear family in mind) and residential theological seminaries, but we might easily add others to the list: single-parent families, people of the same sex living together with or without children, adult children caring for aging parents, religious communities of all sorts, group homes for frail elderly or handicapped persons, bands of refugees in camps, communities of the homeless in our cities. Some households emerge out of desperate need; most are driven at some level by the impulse to survive; many are informed and transformed by mutual affection and generosity of spirit. Bonhoeffer's point is that life together is meant to be a blessing, whatever the circumstances that engender it, because God made us for such life. Christian life is not an alternative to life together, but its perfection.

In this book I wish primarily to consider the religious convictions and moral goals that motivate Christians to take up life together freely and purposefully. If we know what informs the Christian choice to form a household, we will also know where the blessing of life together lies for the Christian—even when the particular households we find ourselves in are not the ones we might have chosen. The following discussion will focus, therefore, on the *vocation* of householding as it finds expression in marriage, same-sex unions, the monastic life, and single-parent households.

What is a household? Broadly speaking, a household is two or more people sharing the daily round of life to a significant degree and over a significant period of time, whether the sharing is freely chosen or not. This intentionally loose definition covers a broad range of living arrangements, from the partnership of two people who share shelter, sleep, sex, food, childrearing, financial resources and so forth, to communities on the monastic model, to people who live alone but whose daily life is a rich weave of shared meals, hospitality, deep attachments, and daily care for others, or whose solitude is heavy with the remembered presence of the dead.

What all households have in common is a very high degree of familiarity—knowing and being known not just with our public faces on, but more the way God knows us—in our sleeping and in our rising, in our going out and our coming in, as Psalm 121 puts it. Whenever we use the word "family" we are highlighting this aspect of life together. Family is really synonymous with household, although its use is sometimes so restricted to households made up of parents and children that I shall use the word household throughout this book.

To ask why Christians value life together is to ask what a Christian household is and what kind of householding Christian faith inspires. We can expect to find many different sorts of Christian households. What role do they play in our formation and growth in the Christian life? What principles and goals inform them? How do these principles and goals relate to the life and work of the church as a whole? By what criteria can we tell the difference among households that are holy, households that fall short of holiness, and households whose basic premises rule out any possibility of holiness? The exploration of these questions amounts to the development of a theology of the Christian household, which is what this book is about.

Once we have begun to sketch out answers to these questions we will be in a position to ask some new and, I think, more fruitful questions about same-sex unions. But I hope that this approach will also lead us to see that the whole matter of householding is something that requires intense and imaginative moral reflection on the part of the churches. The emergence into the light of gay and lesbian partnerships demanding recognition and support draws our attention first because it challenges traditional Christian *mores* so boldly. But there are other issues relating to the Christian household which might seem less intractable if they were reexamined in the light of a theology of householding.

For instance, it is very difficult to know just what Christian marriage is about when most of the social needs that it fitted into have gone away (changing economic concerns, no economic necessity for children, dwindling class structures, greater mobility). Is marriage a sexual union that happens to be heterosexual? What relation then does it bear to parenting, if any? There is certainly no need to defend the fact that the church solemnizes marriages, but as more and more marriages fail we do need to be clearer about what we think the point of marriage is, so that we can support people in the enterprise and help them integrate their marriages with their spiritual journeys. Is marriage about love, or procreation, or both? None of these statements is untrue, but it is hard to see what any of them has to do with the gospel. For instance, what constitutes married love as a Christian task? What is the meaning of procreation (on its own, or as it may be related to love) in a world of contraception and overpopulation?

In the absence of any objective social or economic reasons for marriage (Christian or secular), we are increasingly driven to suppose that this way of life must be commended on romantic lines. But this is to privatize it. Or, conversely, if we try to lift up marriage as the pledge of our commitment to God's future through the continuation of the generations (with all due consideration to the cause of population control), we run the risk of reviving old patriarchal models, since these are the only models we know.

I suggest that we refocus the lens, and look at marriage neither as romance nor as an institution subordinated to the claims of social (including ecclesiastical) continuity, but as a form of life together which, like all Christian life together, cannot unlock its particular goods until we have determined what Christians suppose the purpose of *any* kind of life together to be. We must begin by asking why Christians value life together. This is the same as asking why Christians value the neighbor, that is, the one who is near. The answer to this question is by no means obvious. Some would say we should first ask *whether* Christians value life together, since Christians have not been altogether clear about this. There is a strong streak of the antisocial in the Christian spiritual tradition: late classical Greek culture had a profound effect on the developing gentile church, often in ways that went very much against the grain of biblical teaching. As Peter Brown and other scholars have noted,[2] the period tended to view salvation as escape from the entanglements of community. This often went hand in hand with contempt for the body, and also, of course, for sex, and hence ambivalence about household life.

The biblical view contrasts sharply with this perspective. The Bible envisions a humanity that is essentially connected; salvation is therefore not a matter of breaking connection in order to obtain individual salvation, but of restoring the whole community to health. The vocation of the people of God is, ultimately, to heal the nations by witnessing to the glory of the one God. Such a vision leaves no room for ambivalence about anything that connects the Jews to their land, to their people, and to their families.

The body is viewed as holy, and, as is well known, a real life apart from the body is scarcely imagined. Sex is good when it is fruitful, and is to be enjoyed. The family is revered as a building-block of the people.

This is the idea underlying Paul's metaphor of the body of Christ. The human race is the body of Adam, which is sick and requires healing. The church is the community which is formed around Jesus, who is like a new beginning within the human race. To use a New Testament image, it is like a little leaven raising a great amount of dough (see Matthew 13:33). Communion with Jesus is the beginning of our communion with every other human being, starting with Jesus. This new web of relations is the new creation, the new Adam, the body of Christ. The church is that new creation, growing like leaven within the old and ravaged body of Adam, that is, the human race as a web of collusion. Every member of the body of Christ is such by virtue of his or her actual communion with Jesus. The body of Christ takes shape wherever the individual believer, in the strength of her communion with Jesus and as an extension of that relation, begins to transform her nearness with others from a relation of collusion into one of communion. Every such extension is the new creation in embryo. The church has its beginning time and again in the communion of two or three in the name of Jesus (Matthew 18:20).

Paul's emphasis on non-marriage as an option for Christians, male or female, is a break with the ancient Jewish tradition. But it is not a break with the high regard in which connection is held. Those who marry sanctify each other's bodies and the bodies of their children: "For the unbelieving husband is made holy through his wife, and the unbelieving wife is made holy through her husband. Otherwise, your children would be unclean" (1 Corinthians 7:14). It is through their closeness to each other that they minister the healing touch of Jesus. Likewise, those who do not marry are free to participate even more fully in the life of the community. Finally, the community itself is preparation for more connection, not less. Paul is fond of calling the church a household, a temple of God, a commonwealth—all images drawn from the Hebrew scriptures, and all suggesting that the kingdom of heaven is a crowded place, thronged with worshipers and noisy not only with the sound of prayer but with conversation.

Paul's teaching about connection is consistent with that of Jesus, as it appears in the gospel texts. On more than one occasion Jesus challenges the ultimate value of the household, as, for instance, when he says to the would-be disciple who asks leave to bury his father, "Let the dead bury the dead." Here and elsewhere Jesus is not merely challenging the biological family, but any relationship or personal responsibility that presumes to stand between the individual and her ultimate responsibility to the human race as a whole. But when Jesus does this, it is in order to insist that the household recognize its subservience to the kingdom of God.

Yet that kingdom is about nearness, because it is about Jesus, who embraced connection more completely than anyone else. If the gospel brings household life under suspicion, it is not because it entails too much nearness, but because sometimes it may permit too little. If the gospel exalts the single life, it is not because the single life provides an escape from nearness, but because it catapults those who live it into more nearness. Jesus did not call his disciples out of their families in order to protect them from contact with others. Whether *more* nearness involves the reformation of household life, and whether such reformation involves more or less tolerance for a greater diversity of types of household, is a question we shall leave open for the time being. But if, when all is said and done, there remains such a thing as Christian householding, it will be by way of more nearness, not less. Christ, who begins by offering us community with him, has come not to deliver us from community, but to give new life to the communities we already have.

The tension between these two approaches, which for the sake of convenience we will label the Greek and the biblical, is strikingly illustrated by the story of Augustine of Hippo's struggle with the idea of the neighbor. Not only did this fifth-century bishop understand sinful relationships to be dangerous—that is understandable enough. He also was wary of virtuous friendships, lest their moral beauty draw our attention away from the even greater beauty of the divine light. Thus, in a section of *On Christian Doctrine* written seven or so years after his baptism, Augustine arrives at an erroneous conclusion about the meaning of the love of neighbor. Having made a distinction between things that are to be enjoyed (as ends in themselves) and things that are to be used (as means to those ends), Augustine asserts very strongly that only God (to the exclusion of the neighbor) is to be enjoyed.

This word "used" may be confusing for modern ears. We should not be put off, first of all, by the way in which Augustine uses the word "thing" (*res* in Latin). For Augustine, a "thing" is anything that exists—including people and God. Secondly, we need to be aware that by "enjoyment" Augustine means something rather different from what we usually mean. We tend to think of "enjoyment" as something we hope to get out of something we are using—and so it is difficult to understand what Augustine means by the distinction between use and enjoyment. What he is trying to get at might be better expressed today like this. There are some things which we commit ourselves to not because we can get something out of them but because we are convinced that they are right in and of themselves. Thus an elderly woman with no children or grandchildren might still vote for a school bond because she believes that good education is important. It is therefore possible to distinguish the notion of goodness from the notion of utility. Given this distinction, it is also possible to be lost in admiration for sheer goodness—so much so that one would sacrifice one's own immediate personal advantage in order to further that good and to be associated with it. This kind of admiration is what Augustine means by enjoyment.

What Augustine is trying to say is that there is a higher source of happiness and delight than that which can be afforded by the achievement of personal advantage. And this is precisely the kind of delight we experience when we are close to God. We cannot be close to God and consider our own advantage to be the most important thing. But because God is love, to be close to God does not mean being eclipsed by God—although this would itself be a cause of joy for those who love God; rather, it means getting to be alive in the presence of that for which we would gladly give our life away.

We can see why Augustine would leap to the conclusion that only God can be properly enjoyed. Having made this assertion, however, Augustine pauses over the problem of the neighbor. We are commanded to love God; we are also commanded to love the neighbor. Does this not imply that the neighbor, like God, is something to be enjoyed for its own sake?

> We who enjoy and use other things are things ourselves. A great thing is [humankind], made in the image and likeness of God....Thus there is a profound question whether [human beings] should enjoy themselves, use themselves, or both. For it is commanded to us that we should love one another, but it is to be asked whether [human beings are] to be loved by [human beings] for [their] own sake or for the sake of something else.[3]

Astonishingly, Augustine's answer is *no*—only God can be enjoyed: "But I think that [the human person] is to be loved for the sake of something else." That "for the sake of which" human beings are to be loved is, of course, God:

> [God] has mercy on us that we may enjoy [God], and we have mercy on our neighbor so that we may enjoy [God].[4]

That is, we are to "use" one another as resources for getting closer to God. The neighbor is to be used as a spiritual resource on the way to God: we use our virtuous friends to spur us on; we use our enemies to chasten us and make us humble. This use is still a kind of love (says Augustine), because to use the neighbor in this way is also to commend her to her own relationship with God. By using her rather than attempting to enjoy her, I am stepping out of the way so that, apart from my being used in turn, we both remain free to concentrate on God:

> The holy [human being] and the holy angel refresh us with what they have received, and only with what they have received, either for themselves or for us, and even though we are wearied and desire to rest, and to remain with them, they urge us onward when we have been refreshed toward [God] in whose enjoyment we may both be blessed.[5]

Augustine's argument illustrates two things very clearly: first, how hard it was for a gentile Christian in the ancient world not to view love of neighbor as an obstacle to love of God; second, how easy it is to affirm love of neighbor without affirming love of nearness at the same time. I disagree with Augustine's argument, and can do so all the more confidently because he himself rejected it in the end. In his late work, *The City of God*, Augustine claims that the life of the saints is a social life *(vita sanctorum socialis est)*,[6] because the neighbor-saint is someone who, along with God, is to be enjoyed. His mature formula runs as follows: we are to love God, and we are to love the neighbor in God.[7] The point is that these two loves are not different in kind, though their objects differ. Both involve enjoyment, and in both cases the object of love is an end-in-itself. What we have here is a thoroughgoing embrace of connection. Notably, this revolution in Augustine's thought brings with it a new appreciation of the body: one of the joys of heaven is beholding the physical beauty of the saints.[8] This is further confirmation that Augustine's mature thought reflects his unqualified embrace of nearness, since our embodiedness is the most basic witness to our location in a world that includes other people. We can no sooner escape from the connection we have with these others than we can step out of our own body. Thus to opt for the body is to opt for connection. Augustine even indulges in a thought-experiment about what we shall look like in heaven. If we die as infants, shall we be raised as infants? If we die old, or handicapped, shall we be raised in the same condition? Augustine surmises that in the resurrection we shall all be perfectly whole and healthy, and shall look the way we would have looked if we had lived to thirty or not grown past it![9]

Today's church prides itself on the high value it places on community, and perhaps we modern Christians do not think we are tempted to break free of human attachments. After all, we maintain that a lively parish is a parish that offers ample occasion for fellowship. We hand out nametags and appoint committees to foster community life. We exchange the peace warmly and give substantial amounts of time during services to exchanging news and welcoming newcomers. We encourage the development of small groups and special programs which bring people together on an informal basis. Surely, we may tell ourselves, if the church has had a problem with connection in the past, we are the generation that is pulling out of it! Yet I find that when my students training for the ministry read Augustine's late writings about the perfected world after the second coming, not only are they surprised that Augustine has such reverence for the body, they are also troubled by the thought of an eternity of embodiment. Even to this day, it seems, the Greek hankering after bodilessness runs deep.

Does our very emphasis on community hide a Christian spirituality that remains uncomfortable with connection? If this were the case, it would help us understand why we are so concerned about corporate life, on the one hand, and yet seemingly so unable to think creatively about same-sex unions, marriage, the family, or any other form of householding, on the other. Paul's discussion of the Corinthian church's behavior at the Lord's Supper addresses such a possibility rather precisely:

> When you come together, it is not really to eat the Lord's supper. For when the time comes to eat, each of you goes ahead with your own supper, and one goes hungry and another becomes drunk. What! Do you not have homes to eat and

drink in? Or do you show contempt for the church of God and humiliate those who have nothing? What should I say to you? Should I commend you? In this matter I do not commend you! (1 Corinthians 11:20-22)

Paul goes on to recount the institution of the Lord's Supper. Then he says:

Whoever, therefore, eats the bread or drinks the cup of the Lord in an unworthy manner will be answerable for the body and blood of the Lord. Examine yourselves, and only then eat of the bread and drink of the cup. For all who eat and drink without discerning the body, eat and drink judgment against themselves. For this reason many of you are weak and ill, and some have died. (1 Corinthians 11:27-30)

Although Paul is angry that the Corinthians approach the Lord's Supper as if it were an occasion for merry-making, his chief concern is not so much their rude and insensitive behavior as it is their fundamental idea of the church. We might have expected Paul to tell the Corinthians to honor the Lord's Supper as their family meal by drinking less and sharing more. But this is not what Paul says. He tells the households to do their eating and drinking at home, and thereby suggests that the eucharist be celebrated as a formal, public rite. Paul implies that the church is not essentially a household marked by familiar ties, but a mystery of vast proportions in which strangers and family members share equally and in which there are no outsiders—and thus no insiders.

This mystery is the communion (*koinonia*)—that is, the redeemed connection—which every follower of Jesus shares with Jesus, and therefore with all fellow believers. This is a communion grounded in Jesus' crucifixion and resurrection—an event which for Paul uniquely reveals the impermanence and ineffectiveness of any barriers dividing human from human. There are differences between people ("there are varieties of gifts, but the same Spirit" [1 Corinthians 12:4]), but these differences do not make for distance or separation ("Jews or Greeks, slave or free—we were all made to drink of one Spirit" [1 Corinthians 12:13]). Every member of this community is available to every other member, as the parts of a body are available to one another, each one distinct but all ordered to a common purpose (1 Corinthians 12:15-20). In this community, where a redeemed connection is embraced by all, the Holy Spirit dwells, as in a temple: "Do you not know that you are God's temple and that God's Spirit dwells in you?" (1 Corinthians 3:16). This is "God's wisdom, secret and hidden, which God decreed before the ages for our glory" (1 Corinthians 2:7). This wisdom is first of all the wisdom of God, who created us for communion with one another, and also the wisdom of the believer, who welcomes the restoration of this communion by accepting fellowship with the Crucified One. By this wisdom the powers of the world, which value disconnection over connection, will eventually be overturned, for God "chose what is weak in the world to shame the strong" (1 Corinthians 1:27). The kingdom of God is the realization of a redeemed nearness that takes us beyond privacy and beyond ordinary justice into the enjoyment of a familiarity that knows no bounds.

Thus, when Paul accuses the Corinthians of failing to "discern the body," he is not simply saying that they do not take seriously the presence of Jesus in the Lord's Supper. Rather, he accuses them of a failure to recognize what *they* really are because of their relationship with Jesus, namely, the beginning of a zone of redeemed connection that will eventually include the entire body of the human race. This is because they are ambivalent (at best) about such a redemption. Their availability to one another and to the world Jesus calls them to embrace often looks more like foolishness than wisdom. Yet to reject redemption on these terms is to reject the cross of Christ, the self-giving whereby Jesus is even now available to us in the shared meal.

Yet it is fatally easy for those in the church to turn away from the kingdom by way of a road that looks like the very kingdom itself—warmth for one another, concern for the community that has formed around a particular altar, a particular priest, a particular event of renewal. But if we slip over into celebrating the particular community we are part of, then we are moving down the slippery slope from self-satisfaction with the group we already are, however diverse, to being part of a group that has turned away from the vision of universal connection. In the name of connection the church must always be looking outward. Where there is ambivalence about connection, it is tempting to turn inward. But this inward-turning always comes at the cost of exclusion, and such exclusion always means that Jesus is also excluded.

The problem with the church at Corinth is one that has beset the church as a whole, and every congregation in it, from the beginning. The common life of the church exists in a constant tension between the promise of Pentecost and the danger of Babel. The question that always faces us is what kind of *koinonia* we are going to have—one based in Christ, which is truly catholic, or one based in ourselves, which brings us back into the orbit of Babel. The old alliances and agreements that make Babel possible are still operating in the world, and we remain in bondage to them. It is hard for us to be joined with others in any kind of common venture, including the common venture of being the church, without being overcome by these systems which, like demonic force fields, work subtly to transform communion into collusion. The complicity of so many German Christians, and of the churches themselves, in the Holocaust of the Jews is an example of the Christian community's vulnerability to evil. So also is the Episcopal Church's early institutional *rapprochement* with the institution of slavery in the South and the segregation of congregations in the North.[10]

Paul's solution is straightforward. The church at Corinth is to avoid the seduction of Babel by avoiding too much familiarity in its common life. As we have seen, this avoidance is strikingly effected by removing the eucharist from its context in a common meal. Is Paul, then, reneging on the notion of the church as a household? Far from reneging, he is imposing a discipline on the church which will serve, in the end, to ensure that this household remains the household of *faith*. The formalization of the eucharist is not a foreclosure on the church as the household of faith. It is the opening of a space in which the claim of justice can be heard and the dignity of the alien can be preserved. There must be sufficient distance between the members of the body, so that new people can get in and so that no member loses sight of the essentially provisional character of this community: we are to offer the eucharist *until the Lord's return.* To discern the body is to recognize in the gathered assembly, and in the holy mysteries it celebrates, the reality of a kingdom which transcends our family ties not by setting them aside, but by engulfing our households in a life together without bounds or limitations of any kind.

Nevertheless, the assembly is not the fruition of this boundlessness; it merely provides a place for it. The formality of its worship is like a held breath, an open space held ready for the arrival of the Lord. The church's claim to universality is a necessary check to our tendency to let familiarity be an excuse for insularity, exclusivity, and bigotry. Familiarity must be balanced by a genuine welcome to the stranger, even if the stranger does not wish to be made into a friend. The church in its essence is always city, it is never hearth. Once the church has achieved the universality that belongs to it as the city of God, it is ready to enter into its final destiny, which is to be the *household* of God. In the final analysis, the church as household must define the church as city, and not the other way around, because the church has its beginning and its perfection in our familiarity with Christ. The city of God must become the house of God, a living temple not made with stones, an edifice of praise. The image of the city represents a kind of middle ground through which the household of faith must pass, in order that it may continually be reconstituted as a household on the Lord's terms, a house not made with hands.

Where do individual households stand in relation to all this? Certainly, when Paul sends the Corinthians to their homes to eat and drink, he does not mean to exclude the life of the household from the life of the church. Nor does he condemn the inherent exclusivity of the household. Rather, by demanding that the family subordinate itself to the universal and inclusive aims of the church, Paul recalls the household to its unique role as a place where we learn what it means to extend to others the holy and righteous nearness we have known individually in Christ. The household, for all its familiarity and potential for abusiveness, is a place where Christ can be learned and nearness sanctified. Christian households are simply households oriented to such learning and open to such sanctification. In the world to come, all relations will be, as it were, near relations. But now, the concrete working out of our nearness in Christ belongs most properly to the Christian household, whose participants struggle, despite the risk of self-exposure and dependence, to recognize one another as fellow pilgrims, fellow followers of Christ, fellow members of something which is ultimately of greater significance than the family itself.

The household accomplishes a sanctification of nearness which the church cannot, as a public gathering, accomplish, but which finally only the church can fully reveal. Thus, each Christian household is a mirror to the whole church of the church's corporate destiny. By the same token, the church as the city of God is not just a corrective to the household, but the constant witness to an as-yet unrealized (and for the time being unrealizable) universal familiarity which will be more embodied, more tactile, more social than our life can possibly be now. It is this future familiarity we celebrate as we gather around the altar to share the mystery of faith.

For Paul the household is the smithy where the repair of connection is being forged, body by body, relation by relation, beginning with the relation of each believer to Jesus himself. The body of Jesus must be discerned at home—that is, we must live on the assumption that our households are themselves beachheads on the kingdom of heaven, instances of the new leaven. We must treat our household life as a spiritual workplace where, as one Jewish tradition puts it, the world is being repaired,[11] or where, as we might say, our nearness to one another is being sanctified. This is true of marriage, with the spouses sanctifying each other and their children; it is true of the communal life of dedicated widows—the first "religious"; it is true of single households of the sort that Paul himself kept; indeed, it is true of whatever kind of household we may as Christians find ourselves in.

Thus, the relation of the households to the church is one of mutual dependence and common purpose. For Paul, the household is not independent of the church. The household, which is necessarily small and self-centered, needs the horizon of the church to keep it focused on the ultimate goal, which is redeemed connection with everyone. Thus the household must subordinate itself to the church through regular attendance at prayers and participation in the Lord's Supper, the sacrament of the kingdom of God. At the same time, the church needs the household, with its commitment to and its experience of holy familiarity, to remind the church that it is not a support group for solitary pilgrims.

If we say this much, we have already answered the question, "Why do Christians value life together?" We value life together because we value the opportunities to embrace our availability to one another in the name of Christ, to transform our violence into communion, and to allow our relations with one another to become a living temple of praise to God. Christian householding is one of the chief ways in which this work is carried out. When Christians affirm householding as a means of working out the commandment to love with those who share our life and our goods with us, it does not mean that they think connection can be limited to the household. It means that the lifelong discipline of loving those within the household makes us better able to recognize and embrace our connection to everyone. It is the discipline of love under the condition of familiarity for the sake of a universal fellowship that characterizes the Christian household in all its forms. This holds for all the traditional forms of Christian householding: lifelong marriage, the lifelong, hospitable friendships of single people, lifelong commitments within a religious community. It may well also hold for other kinds of households, if it can be shown that they, too, exhibit the same characteristics and the same goal.

In this book I shall attempt to substantiate this thesis and explore its implications, both for church order and for the spiritual life. Our next tasks are to say more about the biblical vision regarding connection and nearness (chapter two); how householding serves the sanctification of nearness (chapter three); the scriptural witness, both as problem and as resource (chapters four and five); the disciplines of Christian householding (chapter six); and finally, the light all this can cast on our continuing discussion of same-sex unions, marriage, and childrearing (chapters seven and eight).

Notes

1. _Life Together,_ trans. John Doberstein (New York: Harper and Row, 1954), p. 19.

2. See Brown's excellent study _The Body and Society_ (New York: Columbia University Press, 1988).

3. _On Christian Doctrine,_ trans. D. W. Robertson (Indianapolis: Bobbs-Merrill Company, Inc, 1958), 1:20.

4. _On Christian Doctrine,_ 1:33.

5. _On Christian Doctrine,_ 1:36.

6. _The City of God,_ trans. Marcus Dods (New York: The Modern Library, 1950), 19:17.

7. "The peace of reasonable creatures," writes Augustine in _The City of God,_ "consists in the perfectly ordered and harmonious enjoyment of God and of one another in God" (19:17).

8. _City of God,_ 22:24: "The time is coming when we shall enjoy one another's beauty without any lust."

9. _City of God,_ 22:15.

10. Simone Weil cited the danger of collectivity in the church as a reason for refusing baptism (and hence membership in the community), although her faith in Jesus was unqualified. In _Waiting for God_ (New York: Harper and Row, 1951) she writes:

> What frightens me is the Church as a social structure. Not only on account of its blemishes, but from the very fact that it is something social.... My natural disposition is to be very easily influenced, too

much influenced, and above all by anything collective. I know that if at this moment I had before me a group of twenty young Germans singing Nazi songs in chorus, a part of my soul would instantly become Nazi.... By social I do not mean everything connected with citizenship, but only collective emotions. (pp. 53-54)

11. I refer here to the notion of *tikkun olam*.

Chapter Two

Jesus and the Embrace of Nearness

Jesus said, "The first commandment is, 'Hear, O Israel: the Lord our God, the Lord is one; you shall love the Lord your God with all your heart, and with all your soul, and with all your mind, and with all your strength.' The second is this, 'You shall love your neighbor as yourself.' There is no other commandment greater than these." (Mark 12:29-31)

In this text, Jesus combines the *Shema*, the ancient creed of Israel which enjoins faith in the one God (see Deuteronomy 6:4) with another text from the Torah enjoining love of neighbor (see Leviticus 19:18). The high value that scripture places on the love of neighbor, making it almost equal to the love of God, stands equally at the heart of Christian and Jewish ethics.

But it is also true that we can love the neighbor without wanting ultimately to have anything to do with her, because love of neighbor can be interpreted (or misinterpreted) in such a way that we do not end up valuing our connection with one another at all. The meaning of love of neighbor is so slippery that we must be as clear as possible about what we take its true meaning to be in authentic Christianity. To do so we need to think through the notions of connection, availability, and the love of neighbor.

First, what do we mean by connection? Thomas Aquinas observes that the image of the church as a body—that is, the body

of Christ—is apt not because every member of the church par-
takes of the same nature, but because all its members share a
common goal: the praise of God. Thus, this "body" includes an-
gels as well as human beings:

> The analogy of a body applies to any group in which there are
> a diversity of tasks and activities organized for one goal. Be-
> cause angels and human beings have a common goal, the
> enjoyment of the glory of God, Christ's mystical body includes
> both human beings and angels.[1]

What this means is that we are connected to each other (like
the different members of a body) not because we may be substituted for one another (as one atom may be substituted for another) or because we are already joined to each other (like cells in
a piece of wood), but because we are all ordered (or, as we might
now say, *oriented*) toward a common task and therefore have a
claim on one another. Each of us is *free*. That is, we have the
capacity freely to love God or reject God, to love one another or
reject one another. But the freedom has been given for love, and
therefore is most like freedom when it is flowing in the direction
of love. It is fulfilled in communion with God and neighbor; it is
squandered in alienation from God and neighbor. We might say
that the deck is stacked in the direction of love, because this is
where we find our happiness (happiness being, after all, only
another word for genuine fulfillment).

Our orientation to love is also the source of our duty. Duty is
our experience of a conviction that is still true even when it is our
inclination to resist it or reject it. For instance, I sometimes experience going to church as a duty. This means my inclination
(which may be to catch up on work or to avoid contact with
anyone outside my family) comes into conflict with what really
matters to me. More dramatically, duty may be the call to a discipline I know to be right but am afraid to acknowledge. Thus I may
experience a vocation to a new ministry, or the need to continue
right where I am, as a duty. Finally, the sense of duty may be an
indication of something that has been repressed. I once went

through a period in my life when I stopped going to church and stopped identifying myself as a Christian. But every Sunday morning I felt I was failing to do something I ought to be doing. At the time, I attributed this sense of duty to my upbringing in a churchgoing family. From the perspective of my present faith, I believe it was not "upbringing," but God's call to active membership in the body of Christ.

In all these illustrations, the sense of duty registers our sense that we are not acting in harmony with what we really believe is true. Now, if God has given us freedom in order that we may love God and love each other, then, to the extent that we find ourselves using our freedom to hate God and to hate one another, we must experience the call to love as a duty. Even if I manage to forget about them, God and my neighbor can shake me out of my forgetfulness and press home their claim on me *merely by being there*. Our connection to one another, then, is a function of the fact (as Christians believe) that we have been made by God in order to love God and to love one another.

Anyone may lay a claim on this duty, at any time and for any reason. It hardly matters whether the claimant knows what he or she is doing. When this happens, any pretended distance between me and the other instantly vanishes, if only for a moment.

This occurrence, which takes place every time I pass by a homeless person in the subway, is like the claim of conscience. Perhaps it is the same thing. The remarkable thing about conscience is that it is like a voice that is both my own and the voice of someone else. The sleeping figure slumped on the subway platform calls to me, but it is as if the call is already coming from inside me. Before I can gain control of the situation and turn the sleeping beggar into a possible object of my love, someone I can choose to love or not, his claim invades me, takes charge of me, and makes me its object. How does this happen? It happens, surely, because something in me is already reaching toward him, already longing for contact with him. When the other enters into my purview—and this can occur without the other's awareness or presence—he appeals to a longing which I already have. If I resist the appeal—whether by turning my back on the beggar or, in family life, by erecting barriers against my daughters or my wife—I experience my resistance as a tension within myself. What has been repressed is my own conviction that I am made for communion with this person.

This experience, which I am calling the event of *nearness*, is the key to the biblical notion of the neighbor. The word "neighbor" means someone who is *nigh* to me, near to me. This is also the literal meaning of the Hebrew and Greek words in the Bible which we translate as "neighbor" (*rea* and *plesion*, respectively). This nearness is not merely physical proximity. Nearness connotes spiritual and psychological proximity as well. This is what we mean when we say that someone has "gotten under our skin," or that we are "haunted" by a face, or that we cannot get someone "out of our mind." We notice this nearness when we fall in love, or when we knowingly harm or shun someone and then are con-science-stricken. We also discover it in friendship, and in the relations to which we bind ourselves over time: with spouses, children, students, fellow workers. These are simple examples of our recognition of nearness. But even strangers can show us our condition of nearness: our sympathy with a child crying on the playground, our shame and anger in the presence of a beggar on the subway.

We live in a network of connections, many of them surprising, and it is the event of nearness which brings them home. Jesus himself is not immune to these events. His encounter with the Syrophoenician woman (Mark 7:24-30) is one such event. In a brief and unusual foray outside the ancient Israelite territory, Jesus is accosted by a gentile woman who begs him to heal her daughter of an unclean spirit. At first Jesus puts her off, insisting that his healings are reserved for his own people: "Let the children be fed first, for it is not fair to take the children's food and throw it to the dogs." But the woman's wit and persistence wins him over: she may be one of the dogs, but even the dogs eat the crumbs that fall from the children's table. "For saying that," Jesus says, "you may go—the demon has left your daughter." One of the points of this story is that Jesus is himself available for claims upon him which he had not counted on and which do not fit into his plan. The Syrophoenician woman gets to him by claiming a connection Jesus had not taken notice of until this moment: the claim of the gentile who acknowledges the chosenness of Israel and the God whom Israel proclaims, and so presents herself as a candidate for the healing of the nations, a reversal of the curse on Babylon, "who could not be healed" (Jeremiah 51:9).

We should also note Jesus' encounter with the woman who had been suffering from a hemorrhage for twelve years (Mark 5:25-34). This woman is an anonymous member of the crowd surrounding Jesus as he makes his way to yet another healing. She touches the hem of his garment in the hope of being healed, and "immediately her hemorrhage stopped; and she felt in her body that she was healed of her disease." Jesus feels the power go out from him, and demands to know who has touched him. The woman comes forward and confesses that it is she. Jesus says, "Daughter, your faith has made you well; go in peace, and be healed of your disease."

In both of these stories, Jesus finds himself in a relationship of which he had not expected to be part, and a claim is made on him which he cannot refuse without rejecting his mission in its fullness. Furthermore, both encounters make him ritually unclean—in the one case he comes into close contact with a gentile woman, in the other he is touched by a woman who is suffering from a discharge. These stories are good examples of the event of nearness, because they center on the unexpectedness of the encounter with the stranger, the power of the stranger's claim, and the vulnerability of the one to whom the claim is addressed.

Nearness is never something we choose, any more than connection to another is something we can choose. Nearness simply befalls us, and it does so whenever we encounter another person who awakens our desire for communion or (which is more often the case), arouses in us an (unwanted) sense of duty. We are born connected because we are made by God to be part of a community united in God's praise. If we accept this fact, then encounter with the neighbor is something we can enjoy, as Augustine said we would enjoy all our neighbors in heaven. If we resist our connection, then an encounter with the neighbor is likely to seem like an assault, an interruption, or a detour.

Whether we like it or not, then, we are always at the mercy of the event of nearness. Anyone, at any time, can suddenly emerge from the crowd or the newscast and change my life with a glance or a word. Nearness can be good news or bad—the arrival of the Samaritan could have been bad news instead of good for the Israelite lying by the roadside. At any moment and at any time the tactful and protective reserve that we maintain in our dealings with most human beings can be torn asunder, and we can find ourselves, for good or ill, at the disposal of a stranger, who is aware of us, sees us, and judges us.

We tend to view such chance encounters as exceptions to the distance that ordinarily separates us from one another. But what if the occurrence of nearness indicates our true condition—that is, our radical availability to one another? Then the distance that so often seems to divide us is mere pretense—a pretense which denies the close connection every human being shares with every other human being. Sometimes the occurrence of nearness seems to create distance rather than diminish it, particularly when we are suddenly confronted with the otherness of someone whom we view as an extension of ourselves, such as a child or spouse. But the abyss that opens between us is not a distance that protects or isolates me; on the contrary, it is a distance through which each of us looms large before the other. Like the space between an audience and an actor, it is a distance that makes for more visibility, not less.

The neighbor can be neither reduced to being an extension of myself nor dismissed because she is different from me. It is true that we can refuse to hear the cry or the invitation of the neighbor, just as we can deny the experience of availability into which the neighbor plunges us. It is also true that we can collude with one another to "paper over" these experiences—we can support one another in the illusion of self-sufficiency. But however much we may prefer to think of ourselves as independent of one another, in charge of the relationships we make and the degrees of exposure we permit, the truth is that we are always _radically available_ to every other human being, made for living in each other's pockets. Even a momentary encounter with a stranger touches us to our very core.

By _availability_ I mean our susceptibility to nearness.[2] To say that I am available is to say that anyone can become my neighbor: anyone can get under my skin. This availability is _radical_ in the sense that it is something we cannot avoid. Our availability lies at the root of our being ("radical" means "having-to-do-with-what-one-is-rooted-in"), because we are connected to each other by our common end, the worship of God.

Given our propensity to harm one another, it is very easy to regard our availability to one another as something bad. The opening chapters of Genesis read like an object lesson in the danger we pose to one another as neighbors. In quick succession we are presented with availability as an occasion of collusion (Adam and Eve encouraging each other in disobedience); of shame ("they saw that they were naked, and were ashamed"); of vulnerability (Cain and Abel); and of conspiracy against God (the tower of Babel). We may well dream of retreating from human community, from the world, even from our own bodies. But from the Bible's point of view, such retreat is neither possible nor desirable. Our claim on one another is a condition of our existence as human beings, and it is part of God's good will for us. The only solution is to stop taking advantage of our availability to one another.

Yet this is the very thing we seem unable to do. This is why the question of nearness is fundamentally a religious question: we cannot do anything about our radical availability to one another, nor can we make our radical availability to one another _safe_. We are driven to look beyond ourselves for help. Depending on where we find that help, salvation from the dangers of radical availability will be understood as an ultimate escape from nearness or as its ultimate redemption. Christians are called to choose redemption over escape because their help lies in Jesus, who taught the embrace of nearness from the beginning of his earthly ministry until its end on the cross. The cross itself teaches us, however, not to be naïve about the dangers of nearness this side of Jesus' return. We may well approach nearness with what may look like an ambivalent attitude: *yes* to the restored society which is already being fashioned in our midst, but suspicion about the sin which is often intensified whenever two or three people are gathered together *not* in the name of Jesus.

Against this background we can better appreciate the force of the biblical injunction to love the neighbor (Leviticus 19:18). God commands us to assent to nearness. I am to embrace the fact that everyone, however distant he or she may be in time or space, however removed from me economically or socially or ideologically, is, in the final analysis, close by, because everyone made in the image of God is called to the same worship and the same joy. When it is truly catholic (that is, universal), the church is a body of believers who have accepted this universal connection and are trying to realize it in their lives.

However, Christians in every age have found ways to protect themselves from the full force of this command. We are willing to love each other from a distance, but we shrink from the idea that we are truly connected to each other by virtue of being neighbors. Throughout most of Christian history patriarchy has fulfilled this function, not only by making women and children the extensions of the husband and father (and thus effacing them as neighbors), but also by reducing all relationships, including those between men and men, to the question of the power to assert one's will. In our time, we protect ourselves from the love of nearness by thinking of ourselves as isolated individuals and embracing what I shall call the myth of radical individualism. This myth is usually expressed by words like *autonomy* and *selfhood;* it includes the belief that, in every way that is important, we stand alone and disconnected, like separate atoms which may accidentally bump together to make molecules. We are all self-contained, autonomous, and solitary, and none of us belongs to any partnership which is not, in the final analysis, voluntary. To see ourselves this way helps us remain in denial about nearness. If we are connected to everyone, it means we are available—available for any kind of love or any kind of violence. But if we can imagine our "real selves" as if they were enclosed in a secret place deep within us, only to be revealed when we choose to reveal them, then we can feel safe.

By thinking of our inner selves as solitary and free, we separate our "real self" from the body it inhabits. There is nothing more exposed, open to view, accessible to contact than the human body—whether that contact be loving or violent. That is why we want to deny that our "real self," our individuality, our identity, is in any way identifiable with our body. Rather, the body is a "cover" for the self—a shell. The most that can be said about the relation of our bodies to our "real selves" is that they express our presence within them; when we are dying or incapacitated, people may say we are "not really there." When we are strong, though, we view our bodies as standing between us and the world, hiding our intentions and our calculations. I may have many enemies or potential enemies—all those other hidden selves with intentions that may well conflict with mine—and these enemies may inflict harm on my body or even kill it and in so doing kill me; but none of them can gain access to my inner self, my reason and will, unless I allow it.

Current appeals for the revival of "family values" often seem like attempts to get behind the radical individualist agenda and reassert a way of life rooted in connection. But here too we must be wary. The "family values" agenda is all too often a patriarchal agenda, but even more than this, it may simply be radical individualism in disguise. "Family values" has become synonymous with the recovery of the nuclear family as a safe haven. Yet this notion of _safe haven_ goes hand in hand with the so-called cult of domesticity, an understanding of family life which constituted the first version of the myth of radical individualism. Emerging in the eighteenth and nineteenth centuries with the rise of the middle class in Europe, the cult of domesticity attempted to turn the domestic sphere into a sacred and, above all, a *safe* space—safe from the world and from internal strife. It retained certain features of classic patriarchy: the father remained in charge, and only he moved freely back and forth across the line separating the household from the realm of business and politics. At first sight this new model of family life seems to herald a kinder, more humane form of patriarchy: love and tenderness replace social control and sanctioned violence. For all its sentimentality, however, this view of the ideal family harbors even more violence against women and children: annexation replaces control when the identity of the wife becomes completely submerged in the identity of the husband. What has occurred?

Where there were once two complementary worlds, the world of the marketplace and the world of the heart, now there is only one: the sphere of action and achievement, the public world inhabited by the father. The world of the hearth is transformed into a shadowy realm whose chief purpose is to provide the father with an escape from the world into himself and his own inwardness. In its pure form, this myth of domestic tranquillity is nothing other than the myth of radical individualism, in which the family, deprived of its last vestiges of worldliness, becomes the blank screen upon which the father projects his own fantasies about the inviolable, untouchable and worldless self.[3]

Patriarchy and radical individualism are not compatible, since, as we can see, they are based on different assumptions about nearness. Patriarchy assumes (grudgingly) that we are all connected and available to one another, so it proceeds to manage that connection by imposing a strict hierarchy of roles and powers. Radical individualism, however, assumes that this connection is an illusion and nearness is optional—we can take it or leave it. As the latter gains ground, patriarchy appears increasingly pointless and by and by it must fall away, allowing a new model of family life to emerge.

At first glance, this new model has nothing in common with the cult of domesticity. For one thing, every member of the family possesses his or her own identity. For another, the family is part of the world, not something set apart. This new model is familiar to us all: it is thoroughly contractual, with no pretense to safety. Each member of the family is ultimately responsible for herself or himself, and personal autonomy, though it may at times be challenged by other family members, remains the supreme moral value. Yet the contractual model is not as different from its predecessor as one might expect. It rejects patriarchy and promotes egalitarianism—true enough. But the rejection of patriarchy means little more than the democratization of individualism—the extension to mother and children of the father's monopoly on autonomous selfhood. What we seek in this individualism remains the same: a sense of independence and personal power born of the conviction that connection with others is, in the final analysis, a matter of choice. The cult of domesticity offered the father the luxury of leaving the world whenever he pleased, thus assuring him mastery over it, while the contractual model offers everyone who buys into it the luxury of intimacy without availability, familiarity without pain.

Intimacy, as I have just used the word, must be sharply distinguished from communion or fellowship. By intimacy I mean (and popular culture generally means) a certain understanding of closeness which has its roots in radical individualism. Literally, the word means the sharing of what is most inward (from the Latin *intimus*, innermost). From the radical individualist perspective, there is a certain deliciously oxymoronic quality to the idea of what is innermost being shared, that is, being held in common. The inward is, after all, the domain of the unavailable self. It is not surprising that the notion of intimacy first gained currency in connection with the bourgeois myth of the family, the sacralized inwardness of which coincided so perfectly with the projected inwardness of the father's own self. Today, intimacy denotes the coming together of two impenetrable domains of inwardness—an almost ineffable transgression of the boundaries between two radically individual selves. Intimacy is the collaborative achievement of two wills which remain essentially unconnected. This idea plays itself out in one of two ways. On the one hand, intimacy comes to mean the absorption of one self into another, or the mutual absorption of many selves to create a collective self. On the other hand, intimacy can mean a brief and titillating exercise in gamesmanship in which two selves merely "play" at being available to each other.

The problem with this notion of individualism is twofold. First, it rests on a falsehood, for we *are* connected to others and we have no choice in the matter. Second, because individualism is based on a lie, it must always bear within itself the potential for violence. The cult of domesticity offered the father a chance to play at being an autonomous self, but it did so at tremendous cost—the annihilation of the mother. She had to be nullified, cancelled out, not only because of the role she was forced to play in the domestic masque, but also because her otherness gave the lie to the father's pretensions to inviolability. Even in its egalitarian phase, radical individualism must stand ready to replace tolerance for the other ("I will not get in the way of your autonomy if you do not get in the way of mine") with ruthless cancellation ("I can leave you whenever I please").

At heart, radical individualism is the self's bid to replace God: my will supersedes God's initiative. But the Christian tradition rests on an entirely different understanding of the self's relationship to God. Christians believe that God has acted in the past, and will continue to act in the future; all our activity is a response to God's righteousness as it has been revealed in Christ, or preparation for God's judgment as it will be made plain when Christ returns. With regard to the freedom of God, all our freedom is service, and with regard to the activity of God, all our activity is praise and thanksgiving. We do nothing without God, and we are most truly powerful when we are witnessing to God's glory. Such witness is the true purpose of our will, of our power to act, and of our freedom to love. And because our fellowship with one another is itself God's will for us—indeed, it is for companionship in the praise of God that we truly yearn—Christians not only reject the myth of radical individualism, but embrace our connection with one another both as truth and as good news.

Our availability to one another can be very frightening, even in the light of the gospel. But we find our help in Jesus, who is God's *yes* to our nearness and its sanctification. We profess belief in a savior who drew near to us and suffered the abuses to which that nearness exposed him. The purpose of the Incarnation was not to rescue us from nearness or from the body, but to set our nearness right. Through the Incarnation the Word of God has become our neighbor. As our neighbor, Jesus reveals to us what nearness looks like when it is not corrupted by sin, and bestows on everyone who receives him the experience of a redeemed and justified nearness. We are encouraged by this experience to begin, not naïvely yet with hope, to embrace our nearness with one another.

This teaching is strikingly displayed in the Eastern Orthodox icon of the resurrection. For western Christians this icon may come as a surprise. It does not (as one might expect) depict Jesus rising from the tomb, or appearing to Mary Magdalene or the other apostles; rather, it depicts what the Apostles' Creed calls Jesus' "descent among the dead." Here we see Jesus, with the cross on his back, charging into Hades, his arm outstretched to lift its inhabitants out of the prison of death and lead them into the new life he has just won for them. Adam and Eve figure centrally in this picture. Bewildered and amazed, they greet the Lord who has broken down every barrier separating them from God.

Since the point of icons is to bring us face to face with the kingdom of God, it is extremely significant that this icon brings us face to face with a Jesus who is busy harrowing hell. Encounter with the risen Jesus is not, according to the wisdom which informs this icon, an encounter that requires escape from this world. Jesus comes to meet us where we are. That is the first point. The second point is that, just as in this icon we cannot look on our savior without looking on Adam, Eve, and a host of other people, so we cannot look on Jesus without discovering all the other souls who (like us) are imprisoned by sin and need to be raised with Christ. Encounter with Jesus is encounter with the neighbor who shares my lostness and will share my joy. The icon of the resurrection includes many faces besides Jesus', and so is truly an icon of the kingdom of God.

Jesus himself fairly thrusts us into this kingdom; he hands us over to the church, as Paul, after his blinding on the road to Damascus, was delivered over to Ananias (Acts 9:10-19). I do not mean that Jesus hands us over to the institutional church as such. I mean, rather, that he hands us over to the concrete existence of others in the world who have been touched by Jesus and are working their way through the consequences of this encounter. Jesus told his disciples, "Where two or three are gathered in my name, I am there among them" (Matthew 18:20). But this also means that whenever I am near to Jesus, at least two or three others are going to be there as well. Very often this is the greater surprise. Every true conversion story is a story about awakening to the reality of the church, the worldwide community of those who have also embraced nearness with Jesus and are waiting to embrace us also in his name.

Notes

1. *Summa Theologiae: A Concise Translation*, trans. Timothy McDermott (Allen, Tex.: Thomas More Publishing, 1989), IIIa.8.4, p. 489.

2. The term "availability" will inevitably recall Gabriel Marcel's term *disponibilité*, just as the notion of connection I am exploring owes much to Marcel's notion of intersubjectivity. However, as Marcel employs the term, *disponibilité* implies a freely-chosen attitude of availability to others and to God. I mean something different here. By "radical availability" I mean a condition of accessibility to others which cannot be chosen because it can never be successfully refused.

3. The bourgeois family myth has been the object of countless sociological and economic studies, Friedrich Engel's *The Origin of the Family, Private Property and the State* (trans. Ernest Untermann [Chicago: C. H. Kerr and Co., 1902/1884]) being among the early classics. Theological interest in the cult of domesticity, though late in arriving, has been intense. I have found two articles particularly helpful: Beverly Wildung

Harrison's "The Effect of Industrialization on the Role of Women in Society," in *Making the Connections: Essays in Feminist Social Ethics*, ed. Carol S. Robb (Boston: Beacon Press, 1985), pp. 42-53, and Michael Banner's "'Who are my Mother and My Brothers?': Marx, Bonhoeffer and Benedict and the Redemption of the Family," in *Studies in Christian Ethics* (Edinburgh: T & T Clark, 1996), Vol. 9, No. 1, pp. 1-22. Harrison's essay approaches the bourgeois family from a feminist perspective; Banner takes a slightly more conservative approach.

Chapter Three

Redeeming the Familiar

The Christian path is a slow and often painful schooling under the tutelage of Christ, as we learn to welcome the nearness of one neighbor after another. Householding is one of the ways in which Christians engage in this work. Yet, as we noted in the last chapter, Christianity has always seemed ambivalent about life together and Jesus himself appears at times to reject it outright. This is particularly true in relation to the biological family. Jesus is critical of this form of householding whenever its values (family loyalty, social stability, the known *versus* the unknown) range themselves against the norms of the gospel (loyalty to Jesus, expectation of the kingdom, God-centeredness, openness to change, respect for the stranger).

Does Jesus consider the biological family to be essentially hostile to the good news, or is he merely calling it to subordinate its own ends to those of the gospel? Can the family and the kingdom of God ever go together? When, for example, Jesus demands that his would-be disciples "let the dead bury their own dead" and follow him (Luke 9:60), is he inviting them to turn their backs on the ordinary claims and duties of family life? Is he calling them to follow him right out of the human community, or is he trying to reform family life by grounding it in loyalty in Christ? In that case, what is entailed in loyalty to Christ? How would a household comprising parents and children and other relatives—or any household, for that matter—look if it were informed by loyalty to Christ?

If Christianity is about our embrace of nearness, why are the gospels so often critical of the family? This question is best answered by way of another question: what stands out most about family life when we consider it in relation to the event of nearness? Is there then any difference between encountering the neighbor in the utter stranger and being brought up short by the unexpected otherness of one's spouse or child? Yes and no. The difference between the utter stranger and a member of my own family is, quite simply, familiarity. By "familiarity" I mean a certain quality attaching to relationships between people who are physically close to one another or in some kind of communication with one another over a significant period of time. This definition describes family life perfectly; it is no accident that the word "familiarity" is related to the word "family." We are "familiar" with others when they know us well—perhaps too well: familiarity points to the obvious, the predictable and the ordinary ("familiarity breeds contempt"). Sexual intercourse is a powerful source of familiarity. But so are physical nurture, the sharing of food, working together, sports, sleeping together, being present at birth and death.

Familiarity is not essential to nearness; any chance encounter can reveal our connection to one another. But if familiarity is not a prerequisite, it is certainly an invitation to nearness. Sharing life with one another on a daily basis ensures that we shall be brought face to face with each other in all our weakness, our physicality, our need for companionship, and our common dependence on God. Ongoing life together takes these occasions of nearness and, as it were, stretches them out, so that we come to live in the constant knowledge of our extreme availability to one another, as persons who are in each other's power.

Our familiarity with one another is not simply a function of physical proximity, as anyone who has ever been on a crowded subway car or sat behind the wheel in a traffic jam knows. We become familiar with people not merely by being *next* to them for a long time, the way we might be next to any other physical object, but by registering their presence as *neighbors*—that is, as others who deserve our attention, our respect, and our response. The event of nearness is, after all, an awakening to the fact that the other who stands before me is neither a physical obstruction nor a useful tool. Once this has been established, then physical proximity (an obvious element of householding) provides an opportunity to build on this initial recognition.

Whether we use our life together to build on it, and *how* we build on it, remains, of course, another story. Just as there can be nearness without familiarity—I will probably never again see the other driver whose eyes meet mine at the red light—so there can be familiarity without nearness, or, rather, without the acknowledgment of nearness. This is all too often the case in families, where our knowledge of our close relatives can operate as a tool to put them down or lock them into specified roles in the family system. In this case, the same familiarity that reveals the neighbor is also used to keep him at a distance, or, worse yet, keep her close while making her image blurred and indistinct. This kind of erasure, which does not trouble to notice anything about the neighbor that does not fit our needs, is not like our inattentiveness to other people in the subway car or the traffic jam because it follows on the event of nearness, and therefore involves a willful refusal to allow that event to issue in genuine fellowship. In this case, a very real familiarity becomes the occasion for an intentional, and hence destructive, alienation.

Jesus accuses his own birth family of abusing their familiarity with him in just this way. When his mother and brothers demand that he abandon his ministry and return home, he counters with a question addressed to the assembled company: "Who is my mother, and who are my brothers?" He goes on to provide the answer: "Whoever does the will of my Father in heaven is my brother and sister and mother" (Matthew 12:46-50). Jesus is clearly contrasting his own family, in its failure to see or hear him, with the disciples who have gathered to be taught by him. This contrast operates on several levels. At the most general, Jesus is contrasting those who do his Father's will with those who do not. In this case, Jesus' disciples pass the test because they are listening to what Jesus has to say; Jesus' mother and brothers fail the test, because they are trying to stop Jesus from teaching at all. On another level, the contrast Jesus is drawing has to do with nearness. Presumably Jesus' disciples have embraced nearness with him—why else would he praise them for doing the will of his Father? But Jesus' family is not as near to Jesus as his disciples, because, unlike them, his family has not embraced nearness with him. Quite apart from anything else, Jesus the man has not been discerned by his family as neighbor. The implication is that Jesus' family, which has had every benefit of familiarity with Jesus, has either failed to take advantage of it in order to discern the truth about Jesus or is using familiarity as an excuse not to take Jesus seriously.

Matthew's Jesus put it this way in a similar setting: "Prophets are not without honor except in their own country and in their own house" (Matthew 13:57). On the one hand, Jesus' family seems painfully narrowminded: unable to accept him on his own terms, they are frantic to get Jesus back to Nazareth before he makes a public spectacle of himself. On the other hand, their familiarity seems scarcely distinguishable from their refusal to see Jesus as others see him: they do not notice that they are calling him away from people who do take him seriously as a religious leader. Perhaps they are in the habit of "seeing" Jesus in untruthful ways. More significantly, their familiarity with each other is part and parcel of their collusion to resist and deny the truth that happens to be coming to them by way of this son and brother.

Failure to recognize Jesus as neighbor is also failure to embrace the kingdom of God, since when God gives us fellowship with Jesus, God is calling each of us to enter into a fellowship which goes beyond Jesus alone. To embrace nearness with Jesus is to take on nearness with everybody else, and thus to enter into a fellowship that ultimately knows no bounds. The ancient church cast its lot with this boundless fellowship when it called itself *catholic*, and to this vision of boundless fellowship the church eventually gave the name "catholicity." Jesus is alluding to the principle of catholicity when he says that not only the people gathered around him but "whoever does the will of my Father in heaven is my brother and sister and mother." Jesus' family, and the kind of familiarity they represent at this point in the gospel narrative, do not measure up very well against this standard of limitless fellowship.

Is familiarity then the enemy of universal fellowship? Does our care for those who are already part of our daily life corrode our ability to welcome the alien and the stranger? Or (just as problematically) is familiarity the result of a decision to welcome and care for some people at the expense of others, so that the stranger is always kept at bay? I think there is no question but that familiarity always involves a measure of exclusivity—this is just what Jesus is calling attention to when he contrasts his birth family with the community of faith. But we surely go too far if we oppose familiarity to inclusivity on principle. For one thing, it is impossible to imagine a genuine fellowship, no matter how inclusive, that would not issue in familiarity among all its members. Even if this fellowship included the whole city of God, we would expect that, with an eternity ahead of us, we would all achieve familiarity with one another by and by, and this familiarity would by no means make the community of the saints *less* inclusive. (I can imagine us in heaven giving countless friends our full attention, one by one, till we wheel round to the beginning and start the dance all over again.) For another, the experience of familiarity may not necessarily raise the issue of fellowship at all, let alone the issue of inclusivity and exclusivity.

The parable of the Good Samaritan (Luke 10:25-37) is a good illustration of this. When the Samaritan stops to help the man left half-dead by his robbers, he does not do so in order to establish abiding fellowship with his charge. The point of the story is that the Samaritan "is neighbor to" the victim even though he is a stranger. Of course, the Samaritan becomes familiar with him whether he intends to or not. He washes his wounds and clothes him; he lifts him bodily onto his donkey and brings him to an inn; he puts him to bed and feeds him. But this familiarity does not further bind the Samaritan to his charge. He is able to step into the role of a family member or a familiar friend, and then to recede into the background when the intervention is accomplished.

How does Jesus deal with familiarity? Sometimes the gospels show him avoiding it. He sends the Syrophoenician woman away with her daughter healed (Mark 7:29); he makes the Gerasene demoniac, now in his right mind, go home to his friends to proclaim the kingdom of God (Mark 5:19); he dismisses the five thousand after feeding them (Mark 6:45). One of his most common expressions is "Go!" Jesus himself refuses to linger anywhere, always restless to proclaim the kingdom in the next village, too. Even when the risen Jesus speaks so familiarly and tenderly to Mary Magdalene, he adds, "Do not hold on to me, because I have not yet ascended to the Father" (John 20:17).

Jesus avoids familiarity when it gets in the way of his ministry, but sometimes he invites it. The invitation to follow is usually an invitation to familiarity: the Twelve are in every respect a band of companions, eating, sleeping, studying, and traveling together. The gospel of John presents us with the mysterious self-portrait of the beloved disciple, who claims apostolic authority on the basis of his close relationship with Jesus, whose glory he has seen and touched (John 21:20; see also 1 John 1:1-4). Mary Magdalene recognizes the risen yet familiar Jesus when she hears him speak her name. The kingdom he proclaims cannot but be the occasion for boundless familiarity, an endless wedding feast with countless guests. In heaven, the universal church and the life of the family become one.

So, although Jesus does not stay put for very long, he is constantly affirming familiarity by his presence at weddings and banquets, and by the images he uses to describe the kingdom of heaven (as a wedding, a homecoming party, neighbors celebrating the recovery of a lost coin) which consistently portray a life together which is both all-inclusive *and* familiar. Moreover, he himself models such a life. Jesus' communion with his disciples, which is most fully revealed in the Last Supper, is the fruit of a common life whose depth of familiarity perhaps surpasses that of the family as we usually think of it. The familiarity of the Twelve

(Judas excepted) is not restrictive or abusive, but redeemed. Thus, when Jesus contrasts his disciples with his family, calling the disciples his real mothers and brothers and sisters, he is not contrasting familiarity with nearness; he is contrasting the familiarity that is the fruit of nearness with the familiarity that suppresses it.

In the name of nearness, Jesus rejects any family system that uses familiarity as an excuse to cancel out the neighbor and he affirms life together. To meet the challenge of familiarity is to stick with the people we are already close to—if we can do so without physical or spiritual danger to ourselves or to them. The challenge of life together in Christ is to learn how not to take advantage of our familiarity with one another, and this requires that we risk knowing and being known. The point is to embrace our availability to one another, not to hide it. This embrace involves respect for our embodiedness, acceptance of our need for physical contact, and an overcoming of shame about our impulses and emotions, our sexuality, and our physical frailty. This challenge resolves itself into the challenge of marriage and life partnership, parenthood, friendship, and monastic community. However, these ways of life do not (as we might expect) permit us to turn our backs on the stranger; rather, they invite us to learn with a limited number of people the demands and the joys of that nearness that will know no limits in the kingdom of God.

It is precisely here that a biblical vision of the Christian family—and of Christian householding in general—comes into view. The harsh rebuke Jesus directs against his biological family is not a rejection of familiarity but a demand that family relations be purged of their exclusivity and their commitment to private and conventional values and ends. Thus Jesus challenges the biological family (and all its analogues), in its myriad historical and cultural forms, to become a concrete example of the familiarity of the coming reign of God. In so doing, however, he also clears a space for a whole range of possibilities for Christian life together, which includes much besides marriage and childrearing. Taken together, these possibilities comprise Christian householding: a vocation to life together which is both familiar (family-like) and universal (church-like).

At one end of this spectrum is the life of the spiritual wayfarer who appears entirely to abandon life together for the sake of a wider fellowship. But this abandonment is not total. In the fourteenth century Dame Julian of Norwich literally walled herself off from the possibility of familiarity with others.[1] One might say that her life in her little cell is the exact opposite of household life. The anonymous author of *The Way of a Pilgrim* also appears to abandon all forms of householding, wandering homeless from place to place, with no thought but to "pray without ceasing."[2] Nevertheless, like every good anchorite, Julian assumes that she must be available to anyone who seeks spiritual comfort or advice, and the fact that she has situated herself in one spot, well known to all, ensures that she will become "familiar" to the people of Norwich, just as many of them will no doubt become familiar to her. And the Pilgrim, despite his refusal to become attached to any one place or person save Jesus, carries forever the prayer beads of the old monk who taught him how to pray, banking on the claim of familiarity when he takes the prayer beads as his own after the old man's death.

At the other end of the spectrum stand the couple who have pledged themselves to an exclusive, lifelong sexual union, denying themselves any form of privacy from each other. Through the intense familiarity to which they expose each other they learn not only to discern the mark of Christ on the forehead of the neighbor, but may also begin to taste together the joy that will be theirs with an infinite multitude of familiar neighbors in heaven.

A great deal of tension in the contemporary church is focused at this end of the householding spectrum, for it is here that the question of same-sex union arises; here also we encounter the church's ancient insistence that sexual union between a man and a woman should be monogamous and lifelong—a demand that is now under fairly persistent attack. Here also we find the parental family—that is, the family centered on the raising of children. The parental family comes in many shapes and sizes. Its children may be the biological offspring of the parents or they may be adopted; the family may include one, two, or more parents; the parents may be heterosexual or homosexual. The parental family is a crucial factor in any definition of the Christian household. The interplay of the generations is one of the givens of human life: there will always be children, and these children will always need adults to look after them. Also (as we shall discuss in chapter eight), the welcoming and cherishing of children is a primary form of embracing the neighbor. By extension, family life includes care for aging parents and relatives: those who have brought up children are cared for in turn by their adult children.

We must be careful here not to assume that our own ideal of the self-sufficient nuclear family is normative for other traditions and times. For the early church, and even today in many parts of the world, the family, although it is centered in biological relationships, can include servants and their families, household managers and *their* families, and anyone who for any reason is dependent on or part of the household economy. It is worth noting that the Latin word *familia* refers always to the family in this extended sense, and is best translated not as "family" but as "household." It is to such complex systems of relationship that the New Testament generally refers when it speaks of households.[3] But we can surely broaden the scope of the Christian family further to include any form of life together in which familiarity plays a role: the single-parent family, married couples with adopted children, blended families (where two sets of children by previous marriages share a single household through the remarriage of the surviving parents or of the parents who have custody), same-sex partners raising children from previous marriages or gained by adoption or arranged pregnancies—indeed any family configuration or situation that invites a certain level of familiarity among its participants, with all the profound and lifelong disciplines this familiarity requires if it is to be life-giving.

Between the way of the anchorite (or anyone who intentionally chooses the way of solitude) and the way of sexual union and parenting stand all the other disciplines of shared life, including religious communities, single people who share their homes and lives with others, and people who live alone but offer hospitality to many. All these forms of householding display elements of familiarity and universality in differing combinations. Of these the monastic life—itself luxuriant in its multiplicity—is historically the most significant. The Christian tradition has always been quick to distinguish marriage from celibacy, and family life from the life of the religious community, but it has always assumed that both were examples of Christian householding. Religious communities—whether groups of widows supported by local congregations, self-supporting bands of missionaries, or, later, monastic houses—may well reflect the church's commitment to universality and inclusivity, but they also involve a great deal of in-house familiarity.

We tend to see these arrangements as ways of life that bracket out sexual attachment. But they are really alternatives to the unthoughtful and sinful abuse of familiarity in the parental family. What is most interesting about them is the familiarity such households _do_ embrace. The monastic life is life together with a maximum of space between all fellow householders, a space which is achieved in various ways. For the most part this involves separate cells, a rule of celibacy, and a great deal of silence. Yet familiarity clearly forms part of the discipline of monastic life: meals taken in common, a daily routine of common worship, cooperation in work, property held in common. The emergence of the Christian monastic tradition in the fourth and fifth centuries was not so much a reaction against household life in the familial sense as a reaction against the impulse to _solitary_ life which swept through the Christian community (particularly in Egypt) early in the fourth century. The _Rule of St. Benedict_, which became the foundational document for western monasticism, clearly understands the monastic community as a household, and views the monks' life together as one of the disciplines and joys of their vocation.[4]

Along with the family and the monastic house, the Christian tradition acknowledges a third kind of household—that of a single person living alone. At first the idea of a single household may seem contradictory. If by "householding" we mean living on close familiar terms with others, how can a single person constitute a household? I am not trying to play on the ambiguity of our language, which often speaks of "single households" without intending to say anything about familiarity. But it is perfectly possible to live alone and still invite familiarity with others. Anyone who has attended the blessing of the home of a single person knows how appropriate it is to speak of a single person's home as a household: the very prayers we offer on such an occasion witness to our hope and expectation that the single person's home can indeed be a place where nearness is invoked and embraced in the name of Christ. If the living space of a single person is a space for the celebration of friendship and a place of refuge, where embodied life may reveal itself without shame or fear, then we have in the single person's housekeeping a true form of householding. To be sure, such householding bears within it a great deal of solitude, but it is shot through with occasions for companionship and care. We have all known single people who stepped in with hospitality and friendly advice when our own families could not help us. Such people provided us with genuine householding.

Married households with and without children, single-parent households, monastic and semi-monastic communities, single households—all these and more are mentioned and affirmed in the New Testament texts. Luke and John tell us of the household of Mary, Martha, and Lazarus—all siblings, and apparently unmarried (Luke 10:38f; John 11:1f). The Acts of the Apostles describes the earliest Christians in Jerusalem as owning all things in common, and taking their meals together (2:44-47; 4:32). The earliest missionaries seemed to travel in small groups and to form a kind of mobile household (see, for instance, Acts 13:4-5). Paul is proud of keeping his own house and not sponging off other people's hospitality (1 Corinthians 9:18). He even takes in others from time to time—most famously the slave, Onesimus, the "child" whose "father I have become" in the Lord (Philemon 10). 1 Timothy seems to presuppose groups of widows living together, supported by the community as a whole (1 Timothy 5:9f). And throughout the New Testament writings we catch glimpses of single people, like Lydia (Acts 16:14), Mary, the mother of Mark (Acts 12:12), and Chloe (1 Corinthians 1:11), whose homes are centers of worship and hospitality.

The specifically Christian virtue which attaches to all these types of households is the ability to combine familiarity with mutual respect. It also involves balancing loyalty and care for those who are closest to us with commitment to the universal and inclusive fellowship that is prefigured in the church. Christian householders are willing to give themselves over completely to the good of those closest to them, but they do so in the name of a communion which must, in the end, transcend the legitimate but provisional claims of the household. The Christian approach to householding therefore involves a triple movement. We must begin by rejecting the household's claim to be an end-in-itself. This is the claim which Jesus rejects when he subordinates "family values" to the summons of the cross. This first movement is immediately followed by the second: the ecstatic vision of the heavenly wedding banquet to which all are invited and where familiarity with everyone may be achieved. The third movement is the step back into householding as a way of life in which we can learn and practice Christlike familiarity with a few people, in preparation for the boundless familiarity that awaits us at the end of time.

Paul's discussion of sex, marriage, and virginity in 1 Corinthians 6:13–7:40 illustrates this triple movement beautifully.[5] He rejects marriage if it stands in the way of service to a wider fellowship (this is the first movement), he awaits the coming of God's kingdom, in which we will all be placed on a new footing with one another (the second movement), and he endorses marriage as an entrance into this entirely new mode of social relating (the third movement). If marriage furthers the relations of a woman and a man in the Lord, or even if it provides an opportunity for the woman to bring an unbeliever to the Lord, then well and good, let them marry. Otherwise, it is better for Christians to remain unmarried—not, as we might think, so that they can withdraw from engagement with the neighbor, but so that they can devote themselves to the "affairs of the Lord" (7:32).

Paul does not specify what the "affairs of the Lord" are, except to contrast them with "the affairs of the world," which in this case means "pleasing" one's wife or husband (7:33). Yet Paul is not equating the affairs of the Lord with solitary existence, and practically any passage in 1 Corinthians will suffice to reassure us of that. The entire epistle is concerned with life in community, a life which—even if it is lived outside the traditional *familia*—must, Paul insists, be marked by hospitality, nurture, forbearance, and tact. These are the virtues of those skilled in the embrace of nearness. Sensitivity and attention to others is of paramount importance to Paul precisely because the Christian life is not and cannot be solitary—it is from beginning to end a communion (*koinonia*) with the neighbor in Christ. The "affairs of the Lord," then, include such concerns as the following: not rushing ahead to eat the Lord's Supper while others stand hungry (11:20-34), not indulging in ecstatic utterance when there are people present who can make no sense out of it (14:1-33), and not eating food which has been offered to idols if "weak believers for whom Christ died" are likely to be led astray by such a demonstration of evangelical freedom (8:9-13). It is for the sake of a more wholehearted availability to the community that Paul counsels those who are unmarried to remain so. In so doing, he seems to be laying the groundwork for what will come to be known later as the "religious" life—a life of celibacy lived in close community with others who have chosen the same path, engaged together in a common ministry of service to the church as a whole. In short, Paul is mapping out new territory for Christian householding.

But then what are we to say about marriage? Paul's recommendation in favor of virginity and widowhood seems to imply a negative judgment upon marriage as a viable form of authentically Christian householding. Is Paul saying that marriage gets in the way of nearness? Yes and no. Paul does not hesitate to apply the criterion of nearness critically to marriage, and finds marriage lacking on this score; clearly he favors singleness as a way of life more conducive to inclusive fellowship. Paul also differentiates marriage as a "worldly" practice from Christian singleness as a "spiritual" practice. As already noted, this seems to be the point of Paul's contrast between the "affairs of the Lord" (which are "spiritual") and the "affairs of the world" (with which the married must concern themselves). Therefore it is hard not to hear Paul saying that marriage is a selfish enterprise, little better than a hedge against fornication, regulating the exchange of sexual pleasure but containing little or nothing of *koinonia*.

But it would be a mistake to stop here. For even if Paul does view marriage on the world's terms as a necessary evil (like secular government!), he has no such evil in mind when he describes marriage among Christians. Marriage is redeemed and restored to its true purpose if it is practiced as a means of embracing the neighbor. The key verses run as follows:

> The husband should give to his wife her conjugal rights, and likewise the wife to her husband. For the wife does not have authority over her own body, but the husband does; likewise the husband does not have authority over his own body, but the wife does. (1 Corinthians 7:3-4)

These verses are ordinarily and correctly taken to mean that marriage provides an appropriate place for the satisfaction of sexual desire. But we must be careful not to misread this passage as a disquisition on conjugal rights, as if Paul were spelling out the sexual claims two people have on each other because they have given up sex with anybody else. When the verses are read in this way, they seem to suggest that the difference between Christian married sex and fornication is not the quality of the sexual relation but the setting in which sexual activity occurs—as if the setting provided by marriage "legitimized" what would otherwise be fornication (*porneia*). But Paul does not equate all sexual desire with *porneia*. The alternative Paul envisions between marriage and *porneia* is not between two different settings for satisfaction of the same (questionable) desire, but between two kinds of sexual desire that are altogether different. He demands that within marriage as well as outside of it, Christians "flee fornication," and that sexual desire within marriage be informed by and give shape to the same principles which, for followers of Jesus, must govern all relations between self and neighbor.

What, then, constitutes *chaste* sexual desire? Paul does not tell us in so many words, but we can get at its main features by contrasting it with lustful desire, about which Paul has several very interesting things to say. First, lustful desire is a kind of desecration of the body—both one's own and that of one's partner:

> Shun fornication! Every sin that a person commits is outside
> the body; but the fornicator sins against the body itself. Or do
> you not know that your body is a temple of the Holy Spirit
> within you, which you have from God, and that you are not
> your own? (1 Corinthians 6:18-19)

Second, lustful desire is a betrayal of the believer's relationship with Jesus:

> Do you not know that your bodies are members of Christ?
> Should I therefore take the members of Christ and make them
> members of a prostitute? Never! (1 Corinthians 6:15)

We may infer, then, that chaste sexual desire is from the outset distinguished by reverence for one's own body and for the body of the other. Unlike fornication, such a desire leads to a bodily union that reflects the believer's more fundamental union with Jesus.

What this means, surely, is that chastity is distinguished from fornication precisely to the extent that it is governed by the embrace and not the abuse of nearness. Let us look again at Paul's command to those who are married: "The husband should give to his wife her conjugal rights, and likewise the wife to her husband" (7:3). More literally translated the passage says: "Let the man render to the woman his *debt* [italics mine], and likewise the woman to the man." What is this debt that the husband and the wife owe to each other? The word for "debt" used by Paul here (ὀφειλή [*ofeile*]) recalls Matthew's version of the Lord's Prayer: "Forgive us our debts (ὀφειλήματα [*ofeilemata*]), as we also have forgiven our debtors" (Matthew 6:12). It also recalls Paul's own words in Romans: "Owe (ὀφείλετε [*ofeilete*] no one anything, except to love one another" (13:8). Surely the debt we owe is to discern and welcome one another as neighbor, which means embracing the nearness as well as the good of the neighbor. And why does Paul invoke this debt in the middle of a discussion of marriage? Because for Paul, the dignity and point of marriage as a Christian way of life depends on its being able to be a means of discharging this debt.

This is tantamount to saying that for the Christian sexual union can and must be a mode of the embrace of nearness. *Therefore*, as Paul goes on to say, each partner in marriage must relinquish control over his or her own body—but not, as we might have thought, in exchange for legitimate sexual pleasure on demand. As we have seen, our embodiedness both signifies and demonstrates the fact that we are available to one another whether we like it or not, and the embrace of nearness therefore must involve the acceptance of our bodies. This is just what Paul means when he insists that we should have reverence for our bodies (1 Corinthians 6:19; see also 3:16). Paul wants us to take seriously the exposure that comes with embodiment; he also wants us to see that this extreme availability, which is death-dealing in the context of sin, is life-giving when it occurs in Christ. This pair of concerns lies behind Paul's striking claim that bodily union with a prostitute is a parody of our (no less) bodily union with

Jesus (1 Corinthians 6:15). When Paul insists that our bodies are "members of Christ," he is reminding us that our bodies make us radically available, that we have acknowledged and offered up our bodies and our availability to Jesus by welcoming him as neighbor, and that in so doing we have become members of *his* body, participants in the consecration of his own body on the cross. Thus, to be a "member of Christ" is to have embraced nearness with Jesus, thereby becoming a means by which Jesus repairs and redeems all human relationships. If sex with a prostitute is bad, therefore, it is not because it offends against conventional sexual mores, but because it offends against the sanctification of nearness. For Paul, fornication is an abuse of the other as neighbor, since by it the other is reduced to a sexual object and thus effaced.

Paul is certainly not suggesting (nor am I) that embracing nearness with others in the name of Christ means engaging in sexual activity with them. In chapter six we will have occasion to explore the idea of sexual exclusivity as one implication of the embrace of nearness. But here Paul *is* saying that we belong to Jesus completely, in body as well as in spirit, because he has become our neighbor through his own radical availability, even at the price of his own life: "You were bought with a price; therefore glorify God in your body" (1 Corinthians 6:20). But if we belong to Jesus, then we also belong to one another: we cannot have Jesus as neighbor without also having each other. The Christian task, then, is to find appropriate ways to live out the fact that we do not belong to ourselves alone. The Christian life is shaped by this challenge, and to address it is to devote oneself to the "affairs of the Lord." Marriage, with all its worldly distractions (its capacity to substitute family security for the universal claims of Jesus), seems to go against the grain of the Christian task. It is hard to belong to Jesus and to all the friends of Jesus if one belongs primarily to one's spouse. But Paul grants married persons a share in the Christian life by insisting that the couple's sexual claim on one another can teach them how to offer to each other the same nearness-embracing love Jesus has offered to each of them.

But Paul's text ends up being a good deal more generous than this about marriage. For him, the union of two bodies in marriage turns out to be uniquely the sign of the paschal mystery, that is, of the union of the Crucified One with every believer and with the church as a whole. This idea is fully developed in Ephesians 5 (which may or may not have been written by Paul) and we shall be looking at that passage in chapter four, but we find the seed of this idea in 1 Corinthians 6:15. What does Paul mean when he says we must not have sex with prostitutes because our bodies are the members of Christ? Does he mean that our relationship with Jesus is sexual? Of course not—no more than he would say that the widows' ministry of attention and kindness is sexual. But he does mean that there is something in sexual union that sheds light on our relationship with Jesus.

The familiarity involved in sex brings our availability to the fore, and this makes for either fellowship or abuse—even if the abuse is masked as collusion or codependence. Thus, as we noted earlier, sexual union is a particularly powerful example of our availability to all members of the human race. But union with Jesus is an even more powerful example, for although our relation to Jesus is not itself sexual, it includes and exceeds the unitive power of sex. Our encounter with Jesus exceeds any sexual encounter because it is encounter with one whose purity of intention allows him to know us completely. And precisely because Jesus' knowledge of each of us is free of any selfish motive, union with Jesus redeems us from all our collusive and abusive unions with others, both those unions we have willed and those that have been forced upon us. Jesus' nearness stands in contrast to all sin, but it stands in particularly stark contrast to all forms of sexual abuse, from the most intense to the most casual, from the violent to the contractual. Jesus offers us reverent affirmation, beginning with the affirmation of our bodies; the abuser acts out hostility and disrespect, beginning with disrespect for the body. But if sins against the body parody Jesus' reverence for our bodies, then how much more must chaste sexual love signify the love of Jesus? Chaste sexual union is not for Paul a less-than-perfect way to embrace nearness; it uniquely epitomizes it. So marriage in its own way foreshadows life in the kingdom of God, and in the end this wins it a place of honor in Paul's view of things.

How shall we summarize Paul's teaching with regard to house-holding? We might say that for Paul marriage counts as Christian householding because it makes the familiarity between husband and wife, and between parents and children, the means by which they learn to be each other's neighbors. On the whole Paul prefers the Christian life to be inclined more in the direction of boundless fellowship, and that is why he encourages celibacy at the expense of marriage. Because he is ready for the reign of God to come at any moment, he has little patience with marriage as a road to sanctification: it may build saints, but it does not lead directly to that wider Christian fellowship which for Paul is paramount. Nevertheless, in the final analysis he does not view Christian marriage and Christian celibacy as necessarily opposed in the matter of nearness, nor does he deny the element of familiarity that is present in every Christian life. Paul treats marriage and celibacy as two sides of a tension built into the Christian embrace of nearness, a tension not likely to be resolved this side of Christ's return.

In this chapter I have tried to show that the New Testament does not reject the family as such. What it does reject is any family system that succeeds in substituting familiarity for genuine neighboring, and which uses family loyalty as an excuse to ignore or even demonize the stranger. Jesus does not seek to abandon the family but to place it on the proper footing. Familiarity is to be an occasion for the practice of the embrace of nearness, not a means of avoiding it. A narrow familiarity risks standing in the way of a wider communion; it must not blind us to the vision of a fellowship both inclusive and universal in scope. At the same time, inclusivity without familiarity is an empty notion, since there can be no lasting nearness without familiarity.

Surely any Christian theology of the household worth its salt must be committed to the vision of a familiarity that is all-embrac-ing and knows no bounds. Such a theological vision may require a certain abstention from familiarity in the short run, but it cannot be opposed to it in principle. Looked at in this way, Christian parents raising children do not look so different from Christian monks trying to live in community. Parents and monks alike are struggling to turn life together, with all the familiarity that goes with it, into a means of embracing nearness and extending to others the communion we already have with Christ. Both the parental family and the monastery turn out, on this view, to be distinct but related versions of the same thing—the Christian household. Both kinds of household are called to the sanctification of familiarity within the household, and to hospitality and care for the stranger. But each takes a different approach and faces different pitfalls. The monastic household seeks to live a communal life so well regulated that real forays into the boundless familiarity of heaven may be risked. Such familiarity is tasted in the profound comradeship of shared daily worship over time—a comradeship transcending all the usual barriers of class, fame, and talent. At the same time, the monastic household is especially vulnerable to the temptation of fleeing the neighbor. Monks and nuns are called to give up kinship loyalties and exclusive friendships for the sake of a broader range of relationships, and such a sacrifice can lead to individual isolation if it is not intentionally linked to a spirituality that values nearness. By contrast, the parental household gives itself over more wholeheartedly to "in-house" familiarity—that is, to parenting, filial responsibility, relations with in-laws—and must be especially careful not to lose sight of the big picture. As Jesus says, "Whoever loves father or mother more than me is not worthy of me; and whoever loves son or daughter more than me is not worthy of me" (Matthew 10:37).

Notes

1. Clifton Wolter's introduction to the Penguin Classics edition of Julian's *Revelations of Divine Love* (Harmondsworth, England: Penguin Books, 1966) provides an excellent description of the anchorite's life in medieval

England (see especially pp. 21f). The anchorite's cell was regarded as a "tomb" in which the anchorite lived a life of prayer, "dead to the world." Enclosure in the cell was irrevocable, and the service which accompanied it was modeled on the Mass for the Dead. The *Ancrene Riwle*, or *Rule of Anchorites*, a popular medieval text, offers numerous glimpses into this life. Two passages are particularly relevant to our discussion. In one, the anchoress is reminded that she is not obligated to enter into conversation with members of her birth family. After all, do we expect living persons to carry on a relationship with deceased parents or siblings? In another, the anchoress is advised not to keep pets (although a cat is permissible), lest her care for them lead her into viewing herself as a householder! See *The Ancrene Riwle*, trans. M. B. Salu (London: Burns and Oates, 1955), pp. 187 and 185, respectively.

2. *The Way of a Pilgrim* and *The Pilgrim Continues His Way*, trans. Helen Bacovcin (Garden City, N. Y.: Image Books, 1978).

3. For a concise overview of the family in the New Testament see Carolyn Osiek, "The New Testament and the Family," in *The Family*, ed. Lisa Sowle Cahill and Dietmar Mieth (Maryknoll: Orbis Books, 1995).

4. The same can be said—perhaps even more emphatically—of the Augustinian Rule. See the engaging study by Sister Agatha Mary, S.P.B., *The Rule of Saint Augustine: An Essay in Understanding* (Villanova: Augustinian Press, 1992).

5. I would like at this point to draw special attention to Barbara Hall's elegant discussion of 1 Corinthians 7 in her essay "Homosexuality and a New Creation," in *Our Selves, Our Souls and Bodies Sexuality and the Household of God*, ed. Charles Hefling (Cambridge, Mass.: Cowley Publications, 1996), pp. 148-52.

Chapter Four

The Patriarchal Household

The New Testament is rich in positive references to household life, many of which clearly point to householding as a Christian spiritual path. The problem is that we find almost all these references within texts that assume, and sometimes seem to promote, a patriarchal social structure that offends most of us. I refer particularly to the so-called "household codes"—passages attempting to regulate the relations between husbands and wives, parents and children, masters and slaves—in Ephesians 5:22–6:9, Colossians 3:18–4:1 and 1 Peter 2:18–3:7. The pastoral epistles (the letters to Timothy and Titus) also reveal much about early Christian householding, since these texts tend to understand the church on the analogy of the household (see 1 Timothy 3:1-13, 5:1-16, and 6:1-2; 2 Timothy 2:3-10). In all these New Testament texts women are commanded to be subservient to their husbands in all things, and slaves are to obey their masters for the Lord's sake. How are we to make these texts our own without assenting to the system they seem to enshrine?

It is tempting to avoid these problematic stretches of scripture by searching for what lies behind them or by making allowances for their "historical situation." But Jesus, who emptied himself without reservation to be utterly available to us, invites us to know him by taking the church's scriptures—all of them—seriously. These texts, marked as they are by human sinfulness, are still one of the ways in which we receive him. If and when the New Testament writings distort his witness or his teaching, they show precisely what frightens us about our availability to one another: we are always "known" through the distorting mirror of others' agendas and perspectives. Apart from God's own knowledge of us (itself a sometimes frightening knowledge!) we *are*, in the end, the stories others tell about us and the deeds they do in our name.

This is the sense in which the New Testament, together with the church's eucharistic witness to him, is literally what is left to us of our crucified and risen Lord until his coming again. It is of little use to try to get behind the New Testament to the "real" Jesus, because, quite apart from the fact that such quests usually turn out to tell us more about the questers than about Jesus, such a project draws attention to our refusal to take Jesus as he gives himself to us—through the witness of other human beings. That Jesus gives himself to us in this way and in no other (even the eucharistic presence depends upon the community's *remembrance* of Jesus—itself a witness) demonstrates Jesus' affirmation of radical availability. He is willing that his life work should be in our hands—not in order that we should complete it (for it is complete and perfect), but in order that it should bear fruit in our truthful testimony.

But this does not mean that we must approach the scriptures as merely human documents. If we believe that the disciples were truly led by Jesus into the experience of redeemed community, first with him, then with their fellow disciples, and finally with any stranger who would listen to them, and if we believe that his Spirit continues even today to turn hearts of stone into hearts of flesh, then we must also believe that the New Testament is the witness of Christian communities in the process of transformation. Surely what we have in the gospels and epistles is what is left to us not only of Jesus but of these churches themselves, fellowships of people who treasured what remained to them of Jesus (their remembrance of him, his presence in the eucharistic assembly, his Spirit poured out upon them) and patiently awaited his return. We should not be surprised, then, that the communities of the early church were seized by the desire to give themselves to others as Jesus had given himself to them. Their gift of themselves to us is what we call the New Testament—the record not only of the early church's remembrance of Jesus, but of its long struggle under the Holy Spirit to conform itself to his example.

If this is true, we should expect the New Testament texts to bear the imprint of this process of formation at every turn, *especially* in those passages where the distorting mirrors of convention and sin are most in evidence. In giving themselves to us in these varied and often conflicting texts, the first few generations of Christians reveal their resistance to Jesus' teaching as well as their acceptance. It is tempting to ignore any passage where resistance to the Spirit is most noticeable, and for this discussion those are the passages where householding and patriarchy seem most to go hand in hand. But sometimes these are the most interesting and fruitful passages, because their textual twists and turns betray the Holy Spirit at work, corroding, softening, and subverting all remaining resistance to Christ. Since we believe that the gospel calls us to the embrace of nearness, and we claim that the New Testament affirms householding as one way to live out that embrace, then we ought to expect to find the signature of the Holy Spirit even in those passages on householding that are most difficult for us to accept.

In this chapter we will look at three such passages: Ephesians 5:22-33, Ephesians 6:5-9, and 1 Timothy 3:1-13, 5:1-16, and 6:1-2 (with a sidelong glance at 1 Peter 2:18–3:7). Each of these passages bears the heavy imprint of patriarchy, but without them it is very difficult to construct any theology of the Christian household that takes the New Testament seriously into account. Fortunately—or so I shall try to show—each of these passages also witnesses to a new understanding of the other as neighbor—an understanding that does not so much subvert patriarchy as render it irrelevant and leave it powerless. What emerges is a new vision of the household which is neither patriarchal nor egalitarian, but is evangelical, or gospel-centered.

We begin with Ephesians 5:22-33, a passage that attempts to lay out the duties of wives to husbands and husbands to wives. It is notorious for its demand that wives submit themselves to their husbands: "Wives, be subject to your husbands as you are to the Lord" (5:22). At the same time, it is beloved by many for its demand that husbands not lord it over their wives, but love them in the same way that Christ loves the church: "Husbands, love your wives, just as Christ loved the church and gave himself up for her" (5:25). The writer goes on to declare marriage a "mystery" or "sacrament" of Christ's love for the church:

> For no one ever hates his own body, but he nourishes and tenderly cares for it, just as Christ does for the church, because we are members of his body.... This is a great mystery, and I am applying it to Christ and the church. (5:29-32)

The theme of marriage as the sacramental sign of Christ's relationship with his people figures largely in the traditional theology of marriage, as reflected, for instance, in the Prayer Book marriage office: "[Holy Matrimony] signifies to us the mystery of the union between Christ and his Church, and Holy Scripture commends it to be honored among all people" (BCP 423). The author of Ephesians sums the matter up by exhorting husbands to love their wives as they love themselves, and wives to respect their husbands (5:33).

This is one of the most patriarchal passages in the New Testament. Christ is the head of the man, and the man is the head of the woman: between the wife and her savior stands her husband! Some have tried to ease the patriarchy of this passage by suggesting that when it talks about submission, it does not really mean submission in the ordinary sense. In this regard some scholars have drawn attention to the general exhortation which immediately precedes the section on marriage: "Be subject to one another out of reverence for Christ" (5:21). New Testament scholar John

Howard Yoder has suggested very persuasively that this exhortation to "mutual subordination" is addressed to the whole community—men and women, slave and free. Now it is the responsibility of every community member to rule and to be ruled.[1] The trouble with this reading is that it is too kind to the text as it actually stands. It is true that Ephesians 5:21 exhorts Christians to subordinate themselves to one another, but the text then goes out of its way to bracket the husband-wife relation (and, later on, the master-slave relation) out of the general exhortation to mutual subordination: wives are specifically ordered to submit to their husbands—as if to underscore the fact that "mutual subordination" does not apply to them! We cannot get around the uncomfortable fact that the author of Ephesians seems to be taking pains *not* to undermine the husband's authority over his wife. It makes more sense to assume that the general exhortation is addressed to those members of the community who are already regarded as being equal in status—the free men, who are the only ones who really accomplish something by "submitting themselves freely." It is no wonder that this passage does not sit well with the women of my acquaintance.

At the same time, embedded in the passage's patriarchal assumptions, there lies the potentially revolutionary suggestion that the husband is to exercise his patriarchal privilege by emptying himself of all power, as Jesus did on the cross: "Husbands, love your wives, just as Christ loved the church and gave himself up for her" (5:25). In the light of our discussion of nearness, may we not suppose that this passage calls Christian husbands to imitate Jesus and so acknowledge their wives as neighbors rather than subordinates?

We are justified in reading Ephesians in this light, since its guiding idea is the restored fellowship all human beings have with one another in Christ. The author of Ephesians clearly regards this restoration as the chief work of Christ, and he regards the church as the fruit of that work. Christ is our peace, in whom we are brought *near* (ἐγγύς) (2:13) to the *commonwealth* (πολιτεία) of Israel (2:12); in him we are given life, raised up, and made to sit *together* with him (συζωοποιέω [2:5], συνεγείρω [2:6]). Further-more, this new community we have in Christ is not something that stands outside of him—as if it were something he had made and could then appreciate from a distance. Jesus himself is the cornerstone of this household (2:20), which is to say, the community begins with him and includes him just as a building always includes its cornerstone. The new community is one in which we all share equally in an ongoing fellowship with Jesus.

We return then to the comparison of the husband to Jesus. If we follow the analogy carefully, we see that right from the beginning it subverts the notion that the husband's "headship" implies superiority over his wife. For the author of Ephesians, the whole point of Jesus' headship lies not in any hierarchical status, but in the initiative he has successfully taken to enter into a godly fellowship with each of us, and in so doing to establish a new community whose members are as loving and respectful of one another as Jesus has been (and continues to be) to each of them. In other words, Jesus is "head" simply in the sense that he is "first"; he laid down all claim to power and privilege unilaterally, before anyone else did, and in so doing rendered himself defenseless before the world's attack. Nor can we say that since he "went first" he now exercises power over us. Authority, yes—not power. Not that Jesus cannot claim a right to such power (because he took the risk of holy nearness first). The point is that Jesus is part of the community his initiative has established: the cornerstone may be the "head of the corner" but it also is just one stone among many. It is Jesus' neighboring of each of us that makes it possible for us to neighbor one another—and neighboring does not go with hierarchy any more than it goes with any kind of system that separates people out according to rank or religion or ethnic group ("He has broken down the dividing wall, that is, the hostility between us" [2:14]). To treat someone as a neighbor always over-rides such distinctions; think of the parable of the Good Samaritan. So when the author of Ephesians calls the husband the "head" of the wife in the same way that Jesus is the head of the husband, it can only mean that, just as Jesus is the foundation of our communion with one another, and just as this communion knows nothing of rank or status, so the husband is to drop all claim to power and give himself over to his wife as his neighbor.

We can also come at the passage about husbands and wives from another angle. Not only does their relationship imitate Jesus' initial self-giving to the human race, but it also is an icon of the church as the new humanity Jesus has created by breaking down the walls between us. Ephesians 5 specifically links Genesis 2:24 ("Therefore a man leaves his father and his mother and clings to his wife, and they become one flesh") to Christ's care for the church: *this* is the mystery, the sacramental sign. The logic here is not clear until we turn back to the second chapter of the epistle: "[Christ] has abolished the law with its commandments and or-dinances, *that he might create in himself one new humanity in place of two*" (2:15). The union of the husband and the wife is the sacramental sign of what Jesus accomplished by his death on the cross. Therefore, the relation of husband and wife is as free of commandments and laws—criteria of inclusion and exclusion, empowerment and disempowerment—as the new humanity in which all are simply one in Christ.

We may also read this passage in the light of its subversive affirmation of the body. The husband is to love his wife as he loves his own body. What does it mean to love one's own body? It is possible to love our bodies in a vain and self-conscious way, but this is to love them as we might love a new car or a fine wardrobe. Here the body is a mere covering, a way of dressing ourselves before we step into the world. But, as we have noted repeatedly, the Bible views the body very differently. It is not a "package" for the self, but the proof that the self is always already in the world. The body registers our connection with and our visibility to oth-ers. Ephesians takes this notion for granted when it declares that Jesus has made all human beings one "in his flesh" (2:14). This way of expressing the way Christ has saved us only makes sense if we take the reference to Christ's flesh to include a reference to his own acceptance of connection with us, a connection which is part and parcel of the humanity God's Son took on. Behind the claim that Christ loves his body, the church, is another: that Christ loves his own *physical* body.

Ephesians' argument, then, could be summarized this way. Christ loves the church in the same way he loves his own (physical) body; therefore the husband must love his wife as he loves his own body. Now, if the husband is to love his own body in the way that Jesus loved *his* own body, then he must embrace his own nearness to all other human beings, because this is precisely what is entailed in the Divine Word's willingness to take on our flesh and become one of us. For the husband to love his wife as he loves his body is not, therefore, to love her the way one might love an inferior, but to love her as an occasion for the embrace of nearness.

Finally, we can approach Ephesians 5 from the standpoint of the epistle's approach to householding. The image of the household is central to Ephesians because it functions as a metaphor for the redeemed connection which has been recovered in Jesus Christ. When we turn to Ephesians 5, the image of the household gives way to a consideration of concrete household life—for this, of course, is the true purport of the author's instructions to wives and husbands. What is at issue here is the spiritual principle which is to inform life in the Christian household—which is why the passage goes on to address parents, children, and slaves. Now if the household as an *image* points to the church as a communion of neighbors who embrace their nearness to one another, and if the relationship between husband and wife is supposed to establish a household that can itself be a sacramental sign of Christ's love for the church, then surely the intended relation between husband and wife cannot be hierarchical in any usual sense of the word.

In this connection, it is worthwhile pausing to notice some of the changes the author of Ephesians brings to bear on the image of the household.[2]

> [You are] no longer foreigners and passers-by [literally, people who pass by the house: πάροικος (*paroikos*)], but fellow com-

monwealth members with the saints, and householders [i.e., members of the household: οἰκεῖος *(oikeios)*] of God, having been built onto [or into] the household [ἐποικοδομέω *(epoiko-domeo)*] which is on the foundation of the apostles and prophets, the cornerstone of which is Jesus Christ, in whom the whole process of household-building [οἰκοδομή *(oikodome)*], with everything joined together properly, grows into a holy temple in the Lord, in whom even you are, together with others, part of the process of household-building [συνοικο-δομέω *(sunoikodomeo)*], for building God's permanent house [κατοικήτηριον *(katoiketerion)*] in the spirit. (Ephesians 2:19-22, *translation mine*)

In this passage the theme of a redeemed nearness in Christ is further developed by analogy to a complex image based on the idea of housebuilding—where "house" means not only an edifice but also a household system. In relation to the first meaning, those who have been brought near to one another in Christ are no longer like people in a crowded street who bear no relation to one another or to the building (God's house!) they pass without noticing. Rather, in Christ they are fellow citizens who have been invited together into this building and have taken up residence there. At the same time, in relation to the idea of the house as *household*, these new residents are themselves the stones out of which the house is being built. In other words, the image of the believer as a building-block becomes a new way of expressing the idea of a redeemed nearness. The members of the household of God are as close to one another as the dressed stones of the Temple. This closeness produces a whole which is beautiful and strong because the stones are "properly fitted together"—when these people touch each other, it is in love, not hate. How is this possible? It is possible because the "chief cornerstone" is Christ. This means that the primary building-block is Jesus—it is through relation to him that every other stone is able to align itself properly to its fellows and take its place in this new household.

In summary, the "headship" of the husband, like that of Jesus, lies not in any external role or privilege, but in the initiative he takes to embrace the nearness of his wife. The husband who has been neighbored by Christ (for the husband is part of the church Jesus has taken to himself) is now to follow Jesus in the Way—he is to pick up his cross and follow—but he is to follow by embracing familiarity with his wife, whom he is to love as he loves his own body. If he does not already love his own body, he is here commanded to do so. To love his own body is to love and rejoice in his own availability, and he is to cherish and honor and respect the availability of his wife as well. Read in this way, the passage becomes an affirmation of householding as a way of living out Christ's embrace of the nearness of the neighbor.

But that is not all. The husband's act of neighboring brings him into a new power-relation with his wife, one which effectively cancels his role as overlord. The verse commanding the wife's submission to the husband may remain in force, but there is no corresponding verse urging the husband to claim power over his wife. For to place himself before his wife as neighbor is not only to honor her; it is also to place himself before one who, *as neighbor*, knows, claims, and judges *him*. Ephesians transforms the husband-wife relationship from a relation of domination to one in which the husband must take the initiative in entering with his wife into a communion like the one he has experienced with Jesus. The authority to which the epistle calls the husband is none other than the authority of servanthood or *diakonia*, the servanthood of the Samaritan. What is called for is a genuine act of abasement so that, like Jesus, the husband may give his worldly power away, and take on the condition of a slave.

By basing the authority of the husband on the quality of his servanthood, Ephesians does two things. First, it redefines the husband's legitimate authority, subordinating it to the proclamation of the gospel. The authority of the husband is the authority of one who has been touched by Jesus and is willing to extend Jesus' touch to others (particularly to his wife) in Jesus' name. Second, by grounding the husband's authority in the embrace of nearness, Ephesians clears the way for a reconsideration of the status and role of wives in the household and the church. If the husband's authority is grounded in his embrace of nearness, then surely the wife can claim authority on the same terms. She too may have encountered Jesus; she too must struggle to discern in the other—often the oppressive other—the face of the neighbor. What opens before us here is a model of utter freedom, which has nothing to do with reciprocation or contracts, let alone hierarchy or privilege. The model of patriarchy is replaced not with the model of mutuality, but with the call to be a neighbor and a servant.

After addressing parents and children (children should obey their parents, and parents should not provoke their children), Ephesians goes on to talk about the relations of master to slave (6:5-9). Here we run into the same trouble we encountered in dealing with the topic of husbands and wives. The shift from marriage to slavery is quite natural, since it is precisely in the patriarchal household that the essence of slavery—the slave who is at once familiar and a subhuman tool—achieves its quintessential form. And, it goes without saying, this aspect of slavery goes hand in hand with the treatment of women as if they were property, tools in the patriarch's hands. I have suggested that Ephesians' treatment of marriage spells the end of such an attitude to wives by insisting that familiarity must be accompanied by the acknowledgment of the other as neighbor. But if the ensuing treatment of slavery is nothing other than a condoning of the abuse of familiarity, then my interpretation of the passage on marriage does not hold water either. Where is the good news here?

Yet Ephesians' treatment of the slave works out the implications of the epistle's preceding discussion of husbands and wives. We may begin by noting that in one important respect this passage changes the meaning of the words "master" and "slave" by applying the word "master" to Jesus and the word "slave" to every Christian master who, as a believer, is a slave of Christ. With respect to their common allegiance to Christ, the Christian master and the Christian slave are on an equal footing. Why? Because, as we learn earlier in Ephesians, we have all been redeemed by Christ, transferred into his possession through his triumph on the cross: "[God] has put all things under his feet and has made him the head over all things for the church, which is his body, the fullness of him who fills all in all" (1:22-23). What is the spiritual slavery from which we have been redeemed if not the denial of nearness that compels us to dominate and cancel one another out? By the same token, we experience spiritual slavery whenever our identities seem to be erased by the refusal of others to see us as neighbors, which is the same as not seeing us at all. Such namelessness is one of the cruelest features of servitude. Jesus addresses both these aspects of spiritual slavery. He redeems the oppressors by confronting them with their own (the oppressors') availability, and he delivers the victims of oppression from their anonymity by calling them each by name and becoming their neighbor.

There is no privileging of the master-slave relation here. Rather, as the only legitimate master, Jesus makes a claim on each as neighbor, and does so with invincible power through his resurrection from the dead. In this context, it is irrelevant whether the person "neighbored" by Jesus is in relation to others as husband, wife, master, slave, widow, widower, or virgin. Jesus is lord of all, and in every case, his dominion is the exact opposite of worldly oppression—because he makes a claim which we are free to reject even though we lose our freedom in doing so. If we accept Jesus' claim, it frees us to embrace our own nearness and that of others.

This discussion of Ephesians 5:22–6:9 on marriage and slavery may be supplemented with a brief look at 1 Peter 2:18–3:7. Picking up on a hint from 1 Corinthians 7:14 ("the unbelieving husband is made holy through his wife"), 1 Peter 3:1-7 encourages the wife to submit herself to her husband as Christ submitted himself to the unjust, and (to bring forward an idea expressed a few verses earlier) as the church submits itself to "every human institution"

in order to "silence the ignorance of the foolish" (2:13, 15). Thus, in 1 Peter 3:1 the wife is in a position to fulfill the role of Jesus as suffering servant: "Likewise, women, be subject to your own husbands, so that, if any obey not the word, they also may without the word be won by the discourse [ἀναστροφή *(anastrophe)*] of the wives" (3:1, *translation mine*). It is tempting to interpret this verse as if the author were saying, "Behave well, and this will win your husbands over"—an interpretation which is encouraged by the *Revised* and *New Revised Standard* translations of *anastrophe* as "behavior" and "conduct," respectively. But such a reading compromises the meaning of the word I have translated as "discourse." The point is not how Christian wives "behave." It is about what they proclaim about their encounter with Jesus, whether with words or action or—when this is all that is left to them—in the way they suffer. The analogy is reinforced by the text's parallel exhortation to slaves (2:18-24), whose suffering is explicitly identified with Christ's.

The key idea in this passage is suffering for the sake of conscience. "Conscience" means here what it means throughout the New Testament: knowing oneself to have been saved by God's grace in Christ, knowing oneself therefore not to be bound by any legal requirements that promise righteousness by any means other than this grace, and knowing oneself to be under an obligation to minister to others the grace already bestowed in Christ. Neither in the case of wives or of slaves are we dealing with a simple-minded exhortation to accept repression. The point is that the wife, like the slave, manifests Christ; she does so as one who is saved by faith. The ministry of women (as of slaves) is apostolic, and the men who are "householding with them" (συνοικοῦντες [*sunoikountes*]) are therefore to give honor to them as to fellow-heirs with them of "the gift of life" (3:7).

These texts do not condone the domination of women by men or the enslavement of one human being by another. Quite the opposite. They point, rather, to the opportunity afforded by householding to participate in Jesus' redemption of the world through the embrace of nearness. It is not patriarchal domination which affords this opportunity, but familiarity. A familiarity sought in the name of Christ may, in fact, be expected to erode patriarchy from within.

This is, I believe, the situation of the community addressed by 1 Timothy, the third text I wish to consider here. This epistle is centered in large part on householding, and cannot be ignored in any study of the New Testament understanding of householding. At first sight, this passage presents all the problems relating to patriarchy that we encountered in Ephesians 5 and 6, with none of that passage's dynamic reconfiguration of the relation of husband to wife and master to slave. 1 Timothy is a thorough-going text of domination, which sticks doggedly to the themes of hierarchy and control, especially when it is addressing wives and slaves, and provides no signals (like the analogy between the husband and Christ in Ephesians) that a different set of concerns is operating. Wives are to keep quiet in church and learn from their husbands (2:12). That is, they are to keep out of public life and devote their energies to their household duties (raising children, offering hospitality, aiding the poor). Men, on the other hand, are called to exercise a public ministry of intercession for the whole world, "lifting holy hands" in prayer (2:8). The warrant offered for this is that the woman, not the man, was deceived by the serpent (2:13-14) and is therefore consigned to subservience because of her natural weakness. It is also implied that she will gain her salvation not by receiving Christ but by accepting the consequences of the twofold curse laid upon Eve by God as a punishment for her disobedience: the woman shall yearn for her husband, and he shall lord it over her. Thus, 1 Timothy tells us that women are to be saved through childbearing (2:15). Similarly, young widows should remarry if they can, so that they can continue to devote themselves to the womanly tasks of bearing children and managing household affairs (5:14). Finally, Christian slaves are to be respectful of their masters, especially if they are fellow believers (6:2)! Here, even more than in Ephesians, the household seems to be set apart from the main life of the Christian community and enlisted in the service of an intransigently patriarchal order.

Yet it is possible to read 1 Timothy quite another way without discounting its blatant patriarchy. We must take care not to interpret too narrowly the description of the ideal household which emerges in 1 Timothy. Suppose that this epistle *assumes* a general understanding of Christian householding as a way of sanctifying nearness. When the epistle is read with this possibility in mind, hints of a more truly gospel-centered rethinking of the ancient *familia* begin to emerge.

First, the men are reminded several times in this epistle that it is their job to "rule." The job descriptions provided for bishops and male deacons are blueprints of masculine virtue, and both descriptions call for the husband to "rule" his own children and his household well (3:4, 12). Yet the English translation may be misleading here, since it is hard to conceive of a ruler who is not something of a tyrant. There are a number of words in Greek that might be translated as "rule," and some of them might indeed include tyranny and domination in their meaning. But the Greek verb here carries no such connotations. Rather, the husband is told, literally, to "stand in front of" (προΐστημι) his household, like a representative or a spokesperson, one who is present before and on behalf of those entrusted to his care. Who is to say that this community does not understand this kind of presence to be a form of the imitation of Christ—standing before the church, or rather in place of the church, in order to take upon oneself the sin and pain of the church? It might well be argued that this epistle's references to male leadership, with their repeated use of the verb *proistemi*, are an accurate restatement of the fundamental insight of Ephesians 5.

Second, the admonition to slaves not to take advantage of their Christian masters (6:2) might conceivably be a ploy to shore up slavery against the onslaughts of a gospel-inspired dissatisfaction with household oppression. But this is highly unlikely, since slavetraders (ἀνδροποδιζτής [literally, *stealers of men*]) are included in this epistle's catalogue of sins condemned by God's law (1:10). Is it not more likely that this passage speaks to a community that has understood and implemented the deeper teaching of Ephesians and 1 Peter, and is seriously asking slaves not to abuse the neighbor (i.e., the master) who has given himself over to them as Christ has to the church? Could the text not be speaking to a situation in which the gospel revolution has already taken place?

Third, the catalogue of "good works" enjoined on widows and young women alike sounds like a moral agenda that might be addressed to any Christian, male or female: bringing up children, showing hospitality, washing feet, helping the afflicted, devoting oneself to the good in every way (5:10). It is certainly possible to assume that this catalogue of good works is gender-specific—but are we in fact entitled to make this assumption? Like the model wife of Proverbs, the Christian wife in 1 Timothy is to govern the household with exemplary righteousness. There is nothing striking in this, but if it were the main point then we would expect to hear more about the skills and virtues associated with good household management. As it is, every item in this list belongs on the New Testament list of works required of all Christians in imitation of Christ (and, for that matter, of all Jewish men in fulfillment of the Torah). By the same token widows are enjoined, like men, to exercise a constant ministry of prayer (5:5). If we read carefully, we see that we are not dealing here with a division of labor and with distinct spheres of influence. The widow is not safely shut away within her own "domain." She is called to model the *diakonia* of Christ. This ministry will also take her out into the world, where the sick and the afflicted are to be found.

In this connection it is notable that in this epistle women are called *announcers* or *evangelists* (ἐπαγγέλλομαι) of *godliness* (θεοσέβεια; elsewhere εὐσέβεια) (2:10). This *godliness* is a key notion in the epistle, occurring no fewer than nine times in 1 Timothy. Possibly quoting an early Christian hymn, the epistle calls Jesus the mystery (or sacrament) of godliness: "Great is the mystery of godliness, who was manifested in flesh, vindicated in spirit" (3:16, _translation mine_). If Jesus is himself the mystery of godliness, and if Christian women are announcers or evangelists of this godliness, then the women in this epistle are being portrayed as proclaimers of Jesus—more precisely, as proclaimers of the Jesus who has come near "in flesh." Here is a theme familiar to us from Ephesians 5. Encounter with the One who has embraced nearness with us (by taking on our flesh) issues in a ministry of nearness which, far from abandoning or marginalizing household life, transforms it into a powerful agent of social justice.

If we put these hints together, what emerges is a picture of the household as a place where, despite its patriarchal structure, all those who live in it can embark on the adventure of nearness in Christ's name. The wife models Christ's servanthood; the husband's role, reshaped in the light of that model, becomes one of responsible presence rather than rule from above; the slave, whose dignity has been restored in Christ, struggles not to take advantage of the master's embrace of nearness. Furthermore, this vision of the household becomes the metaphor for an understanding of the community as a whole. Far from being cut off from the all-male realm of preaching and renewal, the household becomes, in 1 Timothy, the place where the implications of encounter with Jesus are being worked out and where the patterns that must govern all relations in the church find their clearest articulation. For the writer of this epistle, then, the church is properly called "the household of God" (3:15), to the extent that all its ministers pattern their ministry after the _diakonia_ of Jesus, all its leaders aspire to the representative office of Jesus, and all its members, freed from the chains of abuse and prejudice, claim their dignity with the tact and forbearance of Jesus.

This is precisely the pattern of ministry exemplified by the young bishop, Timothy, as his portrait emerges in the course of the epistle. It is striking that Timothy, who is a kind of textual icon of gospel-centered authority, exemplifies the virtues of the wife and the slave as well as those of the husband. Like the slave,

Timothy enjoys a status that would be unthinkable outside the church: although he is a young man, the Spirit has conferred on him a ministry of oversight that places him in authority over men older than himself: "Let no one despise your youth" (4:12). Nevertheless, like the slave who is exhorted not to take advantage of his new position *vis-a-vis* the master, he is to treat the elders with all respect: "Do not speak harshly to an older man, but speak to him as a father" (5:1). At the same time, his rule is to be that of the model, not of the master: "Set the believers an example, in speech and conduct [discourse], in love, in faith, in purity" (4:12). Fleeing wealth and worldly pride, Timothy is, like the Christian woman, to follow after "righteousness, godliness, faith, love, patience, gentleness" (6:11). This letter effectively merges the portraits of the virtuous Christian wife and slave with its portrait of Timothy—and, for that matter, its portraits of any good male bishop or deacon.

In all respects, that is, save one: Timothy is not, like the women, told to keep silent, but rather to exhort and teach. Why then *are* the women whom the author calls "evangelists of godliness" silenced? It has been speculated, and I think rightly, that we have in 1 Timothy a document attempting to put a stop to women taking leadership roles in the church.[3] Why should women be told to keep quiet if they were not already speaking out? And why should the community (in the figure of Timothy) be told to silence them if it had not to some extent already accepted the teaching and public ministry of women? We are accustomed to assuming that all New Testament teaching regarding the Christian household serves to shore up male dominance and to legitimize social injustice: concern for the definition and preservation of the Christian household is the sure sign of a conservative patriarchal agenda. But I think it is just the other way around. Just as Ephesians' treatment of marriage occasions one of the most radical New Testament statements of the implication of discipleship for personal relationships, and so points the way toward a genuinely Christian theology of the household, so the things 1 Timothy takes for granted about Christian householding stand out in sharp contrast to the epistle's reactionary agenda. The household described in 1 Timothy is the very source of those liberating innovations (such as women giving public witness to Christ) which the author of 1 Timothy wishes to squelch. As we have seen, in this household every individual who has encountered Jesus as neighbor takes the risk of nearness, and so enjoys *koinonia* with Jesus. If she finds in her fellow householders others who also follow Christ, she finds *koinonia* with them as well, whether they are men or women, slave or free. This vision of the household does not corroborate the epistle's otherwise patriarchal agenda: rather, it exposes and subverts it.

If the revolutionary Christian household described in this epistle stands over against the male dominance the epistle is calling for, why does the epistle not reject the household outright? Why does it not call for domination by men, rather than sacrificial presence? Why does it not spell out the irrelevance of women for Christian ministry or refuse to dignify slaves by addressing them as responsible Christians? The answer to these questions is that the author wants to stand for two things at once. The "godliness" of which the women are evangelists is central to the author's concern—indeed, one of the themes running through the epistle is the defense of the church against those who denigrate the body (and thereby reject nearness). But the author wants to preserve this "godliness" as a Christian virtue without depriving men of their old privileges or offending against conventional scruples about women in public life. The author of 1 Timothy cannot reject the Christian household (with all its anti-patriarchal tendencies) without rejecting nearness as well, and this he cannot do without rejecting Christ.

As I have suggested, the domination of women by men runs counter to the gospel, not because the gospel is egalitarian in the modern sense of that word, but because it is about the embrace of nearness, while patriarchy (like most sinful social structures) is rooted in the rejection of nearness. I do not reject 1 Timothy as an authoritative text, but I do read it as the witness of a community conflicted in its struggle to attain the godliness of Jesus. Given such a reading, I reject as final the author's prohibition of women in leadership roles in the church. In the context of our present discussion, however, this is not the point at issue. We are discussing the Christian household, not church polity. For our purposes, the essential thing is that the ideal household in 1 Timothy is about the embrace of nearness. Thus, although it can coexist with patriarchal patterns of life, the household of 1 Timothy takes the ideological ground out from under these patterns, and spells their eventual ruin.

Notes

1. John Howard Yoder, *The Politics of Jesus* (Grand Rapids: Eerdmans Publishing Company, 1972), pp. 163-92.

2. This passage is full of plays on the word for household (οἰκοζ [*oikos*] or οἰκία [*oikia*]). The word-play is difficult to render in English, but I have tried to bring them out by translating the Greek as literally as possible.

3. In *In Memory of Her: A Feminist Theological Reconstruction of Christian Origins* (New York: Crossroads, 1989 [1983]), pp. 245f, Elisabeth Schussler-Fiorenza argues strongly for such a reading of the pastoral epistles. So also David C. Verner in *The Household of God: The Social World of the Pastoral Epistles* (Chico, Calif.: Scholars Press, 1983), pp. 182f. Many commentators who do not "side" with those elements of the community who seem to lie under 1 Timothy's condemnation recognize that the texts represent a reaction, even if they applaud it. Thus Philip Towner, in *1-2 Timothy and Titus* (Downers Grove, Ill.: InterVarsity Press, 1994), admits that the texts are reactionary, but excuses them on the grounds that "sensitivity to the surrounding [i.e., patriarchal] culture was an important feature of early Christian ethical teaching" (p. 62). Alternatively, Frances Young suggests that the pastorals reflect neither a desire to placate the surrounding pagan culture nor a reaction against anti-patriarchal elements within the church, but a consensus of opinion against outside forces tempting the Christian communities to an unbiblical and anti-worldly asceticism. See her study *The Theology of the Pastoral Letters* (Cambridge: Cambridge University Press, 1994), pp. 13-20.

Chapter Five

Care in the Christian Household

As the New Testament envisions it, the kingdom of God will involve us in boundless sociability; there is no one we will not be close to in heaven. Among other things, Christian life is a schooling in holy familiarity. But this schooling is tricky since, given our weakness and our tendency toward sinfulness, we cannot simply enjoy familiarity with everyone as if we were already in heaven. We must practice Christlike familiarity with a few people in order that we may be ready, when the time comes, to enjoy it with countless others. Of course, our familiarity with a few may cause us to forget the wideness of Christian fellowship, and we may use it as an excuse to ignore the needs of the stranger who comes to the door for help. Thus, we need to be humble enough to minimize the number of people with whom we are familiar, and faithful enough to remain loyal to the universal fellowship which Jesus proclaimed and which our householding is meant to train us for.

Given the need for Christians to balance these two claims, it is not surprising that Christian householding takes many forms. The Christian household is a dynamic working out of the interplay between familiarity (with all its tendencies toward parochialism and narrowness) and universality (with all its tendencies to prefer an abstract humanitarianism to the concrete challenges of being a neighbor). Marriage and parenting constitute one form of Christian householding, but so do the monastic life and the single life. Each of these ways of householding has its own distinct features and graces. But if each way truly is an instance of a single practice—the practice of Christian householding as a means of making Jesus' neighboring our own—then marriage and family, monasticism, singleness, and any other form of Christian life together must share common features and be informed by common standards. We should expect to discern these common themes whenever we consider the Christian household in any form. This is especially so when it comes to the New Testament texts we considered in chapter four. Ephesians 5-6, 1 Peter 2-3, and 1 Timothy all present themselves as texts about marriage and family. The family they deal with is of a very particular sort, however: it is the patriarchal and (if it is wealthy enough) the slaveholding family of the ancient Roman world. But when we read these texts critically, the vision that slowly emerges does not have to do with any kind of family in particular, but with the moral convictions that for Christians must govern and inform familiar relations of any sort. In other words, these texts apply the gospel of Jesus Christ to the condition of familiarity. The result is not a blueprint for the Christian family. It is a window onto God's vision for householding in all its forms.

In this chapter and the next we will begin to identify the moral principles—the basic attitudes, disciplines, and rules of life—implicit in this vision. Although moral principles are always abstractions—attempts to formulate and simplify the far more complicated and knotty patterns of our moral experience—the attempt to articulate such principles is useful. It forces us to see past the particular to the essential. When we strip away the variables, what do all Christian households have in common? What is required of every Christian householder, regardless of his or her particular situation? What makes for the genuine embrace of nearness, and what stands in the way of it? When we ask such questions we are not shying away from the fact that the lives real people make with each other are always unique. On the contrary, we are attempting to achieve the clarity we need in order to look with fresh eyes on the actual households that surround us on every side. The aim is not to codify or institutionalize, but to gain a perspective from which we can discern the Christian discipleship involved in householding even where we do not expect to find it. In this spirit, this chapter will explore the New Testament understanding of "care" or "anxiety" (*merimna* in Greek) as the characteristic attitude of Christian love of neighbor, particularly as this is played out in the household. In chapter six I shall describe the nine basic disciplines of Christian householding: bodily fellowship, exclusivity, accountability to the church, permanence, equality, nonviolence, generosity, hospitality, and nurture.

We may begin by looking once again at the New Testament approach to familiarity. "Familiarity" names the kind of insight we have into one another when we live and work closely together for a long time. By extension, it also refers to the stake we have in each other because of that history. Let us look once again at 1 Corinthians 7, where Paul advises the unmarried members of his flock to choose a life that is less intensely familiar than marriage:

> Concerning virgins....I think that, in view of the impending crisis, it is well for you to remain as you are. Are you bound to a wife? Do not seek to be free. Are you free from a wife? Do not seek a wife. But if you marry, you do not sin, and if a virgin marries, she does not sin. Yet those who marry will experience distress in this life, and I would spare you that. (7:25-28)

For Paul the married life is full of *merimna*, variously translated as anxiety, care, or taking thought. Paul also uses the verb *merimnao*, which means "to be anxious." The married person, as Paul observes a few verses later, is beset by the need to please and, one supposes, to protect and sustain the spouse. "I want you to be free from anxieties," writes Paul.

> The unmarried man is anxious about the affairs of the Lord, how to please the Lord; but the married man is anxious [*merimnao*] about the affairs of the world, how to please his wife, and his interests are divided. And the unmarried woman

and the virgin are anxious about the affairs of the Lord, so that they may be holy in body and spirit; but the married woman is anxious about the affairs of the world, how to please her husband. (7:32-35)

As contrasted with the "carelessness" of the unmarried and unattached, this care has a negative ring, reminding us, perhaps, of the worldly *merimna* deprecated by Jesus in several gospel passages. For instance, in Matthew Jesus says:

Do not worry [*merimnao*] about your life, what you will eat or what you will drink, or about your body, what you will wear. Is not life more than food, and the body more than clothing?...Therefore do not worry, saying, "What will we eat?" or "What will we drink?" or "What will we wear?" For it is the Gentiles who strive for all these things. (Matthew 6:25, 31-32; see also the parallel passage in Luke 12:22f)

Nevertheless, I would like to suggest that in his notion of *merimna*, which I shall simply refer to as "care," Paul provides us with the first principle of Christian householding. We will need to spend some time considering Paul's use of the word more closely.

We might easily think that when Paul speaks of the care of marriage he has in mind something like "distractedness," or even "fussiness," something just this side of the comic. On such a reading, the anxiousness of conjugal familiarity contrasts unfavorably with the calm otherworldliness of dedicated virginity. This is certainly the way many have interpreted the story of Martha and Mary (Luke 10:38-42)—another place where the New Testament seems to pit the anxiety and care of domestic life against the repose that seems to go with attending to "the affairs of the Lord." In this passage, Mary's calm attention to the teaching of Jesus is contrasted to Martha's distraction, and Martha gets the short end of the stick: "Martha, Martha," says Jesus, responding to her complaint that Mary has left her with all the work, "you are worried (*merimnao*) and distracted by many things; there is need of only one thing. Mary has chosen the better part" (Luke 10:41-

42). Yet why is it so often assumed that Jesus is telling Martha not to be anxious about *anything*? And why do we suppose that Mary, sitting at the feet of Jesus, is relieved of care? If we simply take Jesus' words at face value, he is telling Martha that there is only one thing worth being anxious about (or distracted by), and that, presumably, is—what? The word of God? The teaching of Jesus? Familiarity with Jesus himself? Not surprisingly, I suspect it is the last, since familiarity with Jesus—staying close by him, paying attention to him—includes being anxious to hear and obey the word of God and the teaching of Jesus. The point is not a contrast between calmness and *merimna*, but what deserves our attention and what does not.

The same is true when it comes to Paul's understanding of care. We are bound to misread Paul on the relative merits of marriage and virginity if we forget that for him these two ways of life represent the claims of familiarity and universal fellowship, re-spectively, and that these claims interpenetrate and inform each other. What troubles Paul about marriage is that it may draw the spouses' attention away from the wider affairs of the church. He does not intend to suggest that these wider affairs are not an occasion for care. Certainly Paul thinks of care as the charac-teristic preoccupation of the life of familiarity. But we know that for Paul familiarity is also a necessary ingredient in the ministry of the unmarried, and so we should not accuse him of inconsis-tency when he seems to suggest that "being anxious" is a feature of the unmarried life as well. Paul may describe the married person as one who "is anxious" about "the affairs of this world," but he uses precisely the same verb (*merimnao*) to describe the unmarried person's concern for "the affairs of the Lord." Lest we think that in this latter sense being anxious does not have other people (like spouses and other neighbors) as its object, we need only turn to 1 Corinthians 12, where Paul, likening the believing community to a body, describes how the members lavish honor upon one another, and the greatest honor upon the lowliest, in order that "the members may have the same care (*merimnao*) for one another" (12:25). Similarly, Paul commends Timothy to the

Christians at Philippi as one "who will be genuinely concerned (*merimnao*) for [their] welfare" (Philippians 2:20), and in 2 Corinthians he commends himself as one who deals daily with "anxiety (*merimna)* for all the churches" (11:28).

Clearly, care does not belong to marriage alone. For the Christian, Paul might say, familiarity and care are inseparable, and, since the Christian way always involves familiarity, the Christian life also always involves care. It is a feature of all Christian relations. Nor does Paul disparage or mock it. Care is not about being frantic or distracted about someone or something; it describes an inclination of the heart to protect and preserve the well-being and dignity of a brother or sister for whom Christ died, and it finds its wellspring in the believer's familiarity and solidarity with Jesus. This is why the life of the unattached apostle turns out to be, for Paul, every bit as care-filled as the life of the married person who stays at home. To be sure, the way that care is provided in these two kinds of life is not the same. The point about marriage is that it involves intense familiarity with one other person, whereas the single life minimizes familiarity with others for the time being, in order to maximize ministry to strangers. But, as we saw in chapter three, the single person in fact does not give up familiarity entirely. On the one hand, a certain amount of familiarity is bound to accompany anyone's participation in the common life of the church. On the other hand, the disciple who has foresworn the familiarity of household life clings all the more to familiarity with Jesus. The sole care is to please Jesus, and it is perhaps almost beside the point that what pleases Jesus most is that the nearness of every neighbor should be embraced. Thus, although Paul is beset by anxiety "for all the churches," he experiences this anxiety as "care for the affairs of the Lord."

Paul's treatment of the notion of *merimna* gives us yet another way to understand how Paul both distinguishes and combines these different forms of care. For the unmarried, familiarity with others besides Jesus is minimized, and care for them is experienced indirectly as care for what matters to Jesus. In married households, the circle of familiarity extends beyond or flows out from the believer's relationship with Jesus to include others, who in turn become the direct objects of the believer's care. We begin with Jesus, and our hearts move out from there. Of course, Paul is afraid that in the exercise of care, whether by the unmarried or within the context of marriage, Jesus will be forgotten. He is right to be afraid—it is easy for such attachments to turn our hearts away from the reign of God. Again, this is the thrust of Jesus' critique of an uncritical allegiance to "family values." Yet even if Paul is concerned lest private households drift away from Christ, this does not prevent him from recognizing as something holy that care whereby the love we have known in Jesus is applied to our immediate household (spouse, family, convent, circle of friends).

Where genuine care is exercised in the context of familiarity, there the Christian household may be found. Can we define this care more clearly? In classical Christian moral theology, we would say that care is a "disposition," that is, a certain "habit of the heart" (to borrow de Tocqueville's fine phrase) which inclines us to one set of actions rather than another. Care is the disposition to "stick by" those who are already familiar to us, and possibly to take on the burden of familiarity with strangers, in order that we may grow in our capacity for neighborly love. To define it more precisely, *care is the working out of the embrace of nearness, through familiarity with a limited number of people, in the name of nearness with all, under the condition of sin.* I will take up each element of this definition in turn.

Care is the working out of the embrace of nearness. Care takes the abstract idea of neighborly love (the same thing as infinite regard for the neighbor) and makes it real. When I have Christian care for someone, I am giving myself over to that person's absolute claim on me. The burden of obligation and concern which then possesses me is precisely what Paul means when he says that married people are full of anxiety for their spouses.

Care makes the embrace of nearness real through familiarity with a limited number of people. Regard for the neighbor embodies itself in an anxious and often preoccupying concern for the physical and spiritual welfare of a few persons. Far from mere well-wishing, or even generous support from afar, care is the concrete devotion of time, resources, labor, and presence. It involves transmitting to others the love we have known in being touched by Jesus. Since our own reconciliation with God and the neighbor has been brought about through Jesus' own "hands on" ministry to our souls and bodies, our own ministry of reconciliation must also be "hands on." But only Jesus can attend completely to every human being. We are limited by our location in space and time, and by the uphill fight each of us must wage against our chronic resistance to the neighbor. So, for most of us, working out our salvation in fear and trembling means walking the way of familiarity, and, because we cannot be familiar with everybody, this means giving ourselves over to care for a limited number of people.

This element of limitation is an important feature of any healthy household, and certainly figures in the definition of the Christian household. Households imply boundaries—boundaries that we draw around our housemates to distinguish them from all the rest of our neighbors. This does not mean that we can second-guess where those boundaries will be drawn and what they will look like. The difference between the private household and the wider community is relative, not absolute. Paul and his followers refer often to the Christian community as "the family of faith" or the "household of God," and in so doing lift up the element of familiar care which even today is an important dimension of parish life. When parishioners visit other parishioners who are sick, or take the trouble to know the names of the children in Sunday school, or comfort a grieving widow in the coffee hour, they are exhibiting a ministry of care which stands at the heart of any healthy congregation's life. This ministry of care is what Paul calls the Galatians to when he tells them to "bear one another's burdens, and in this way you will fulfill the law of Christ" (Galatians 6:2). When he goes on to exhort them to "work for the good of all, and especially for those of the family of faith" (6:10), he is not relieving them of their duty to the stranger and the nonbeliever, but warning them not to let an abstract idea of universal fellowship substitute for the genuine care owed to the neighbor who is already there.

Christian fellowship cannot escape this tension between the far off and the near. But, as we have seen, familiarity need not stand opposed to universality. It is necessary to live out the embrace of nearness with a few in anticipation of the limitless fellowship that our faith teaches us to expect in the world to come. This brings us to the third element in the definition of care.

Care is exercised in the name of nearness with all. Care must focus both on the present welfare of one's familiar neighbors—the child, the spouse, the brother monk, the aging parent, the friend—and on their place at the Lamb's wedding feast. The church's anticipation of that feast is a source of creative anxiety in its own right. These two spheres of concern—one unavoidably narrow, the other inescapably vast—are two inseparable dimensions of the same care; one informs the other. For instance, if I am possessed of genuine care for my wife and children, I will be reminded constantly that they are also my fellow pilgrims on the way of the cross. But my care for them as fellow pilgrims will not diminish my delight that they happen to be my *family!* Care breaks through our habitual shortsightedness about those closest to us, not in order to shake off familiarity but to reestablish it on a proper foundation. The profound attachment I share with my family is not rendered irrelevant by the fact that we are all destined to enjoy an equally profound attachment to billions of others as well. Christian care is itself productive of familiarity, ever transforming the old familiarity into a new familiarity which is itself the reign of God in our midst.

Care is exercised under the condition of sin. Were it not for our consciousness of sin, our own sin and that of others, we would not succumb so willingly to the insular and self-centered tendencies of our households, nor would we need to be so watchful of our inclination to use the household as an excuse to ignore Jesus' call to follow him. It is because of sin that care is an anxious and not a serene *yes* to God's command. Our lives are full of spiritual anxiety, and appropriately so, because, although our salvation is assured in Christ, our sanctification is not yet complete.

We are called—or perhaps pushed—by Jesus to turn with him to other neighbors. But we know that in making our response to this call, our inclination to sin spells almost certain risk to others and ourselves. Against the background of this risk care reveals its true complexity and richness. Viewed in this light, care names the Christian householder's response to a fourfold challenge. To begin with, we must struggle to achieve household relationships that do not shut out God. I am not speaking here of the way in which attachment to family can blind us to the wider scope of the gospel, although, as we have seen, this concern certainly underlies Jesus' apparent attacks on family life. I am speaking of the way in which an outright rejection of God's truth and God's command can masquerade under the cloak of Christian householding. Genuine Christian familiarity means the embrace of nearness by all members of the household. It is all too easy, however, for two or more members of a household to enable each other in their flight from nearness. When we help each other to make idols of drugs or money or social status, we are in danger of conspiring to turn our back on God's truth. Collusion against God can take the form of codependency; it can also take the form of a false moralism, like that of Christian families in Nazi Germany that failed to protest the destruction of Jewish lives because they believed they must place the safety of their own children first.[1]

In the second place, care is an expression of the believer's struggle against inattentiveness. We are not only to glance at the neighbor and look away, but to *attend* to the neighbor—otherwise how can we ever see past our own prejudices about one another and the distortions of our own projections? In her famous collection of essays, *Waiting for God*, Simone Weil asserts that attention is the cardinal Christian virtue because it requires a self-forgetfulness and a focus on the other which for her epitomize Christian love:

> Not only does the love of God have attention for its substance; the love of our neighbor, which we know to be the same love, is made of this same substance. Those who are unhappy have no need for anything in this world but people capable of giving them their attention. The capacity to give one's attention to a sufferer is a very rare and difficult thing; it is almost a miracle; it is a miracle. Nearly all those who think they have this capacity do not possess it. Warmth of heart, impulsiveness, pity are not enough.[2]

For the Christian householder, this means overcoming the inertia and carelessness that may accompany familiarity: often it is easier to pay attention to strangers than to the members of one's own family. It is not quite right to suggest that familiarity itself dulls or deadens our awareness—since very often the intention to become familiar invites nearness, while the achievement of familiarity prolongs it. But it is possible to use our past knowledge of others to keep ourselves from ever learning anything new. When we abuse our knowledge of one another in this way, familiarity becomes a veil we throw over the neighbor rather than an occasion for encounter. At its most basic, care shows itself as the determination to overcome the temptation to brace ourselves against the full impact that our fellow householder has on our lives. In a sense, the whole work of sanctification begins here. If I do not discern the neighbor in my wife and children during the ordinary round of our household life, I am not likely to discern the neighbor in someone whom I hardly know.

If caring involves the challenge of paying attention, it involves still more the challenge of touching without harming. If my refusal to recognize the nearness of the other fails to shut out the neighbor's claim on me, my rejection of that claim may lead me to take advantage of the neighbor's own availability while denying my own. Violence denotes any act whereby I betray the neighbor's accessibility to me and wrongfully *avail* myself of it. Such violation can take many forms—physical, sexual, and psychological. All forms of violence, including the psychological, constitute an attack on the neighbor's body, because (as we discussed in chapter two) our bodies locate us in the world, and it is in them that we experience our availability to the world.

This will be evident if we reflect for a moment on what it feels like to be ridiculed. We register the spiritual attack of ridicule with a physical response (cheeks flushing, voice choked, knees weak), and this experience may cause us to identify with our bodies more than usual. Consider, for example, the classic example of the Little Leaguer who cannot hit the ball during a game, and is subject to the remarks of the opposing team—or worse, of his or her own teammates. Anyone who has undergone this or a comparable set of public humiliations knows that the experience is a profoundly physical one—even if the ridicule is entirely verbal. One feels the sensation of being pulled down into one's body and thrust visibly and miserably into the public glare. Why does shame make us so aware of our bodies? Is it not because shame is an encounter with our radical availability? When we say we feel shame, we mean that we have been exposed under hostile circumstances and are unable to hide. Indeed, we may feel that our very bodies have betrayed us: If only I had not begun to shake! If only my heart had not begun to beat so fast! But the shock of our exposure would not be registered so intensely in our bodies—we would not feel that our bodies were the cinema screen on which our souls' secrets were writ large—if we had not long ago associated our bodies with our radical availability. The two things go together.

Violence is an attack on the body—but ridicule counts as such an attack. Beneath the idea of physical violence lies the root of all the crimes we commit against one another, namely, the manipulation of each others' susceptibility to shame, whether through overt physical or sexual attack upon the body, or through more subtle attacks upon our dignity, which we then experience in intensely physical ways.

Obviously, care involves abstaining from violence. But here again we must not overlook the element of struggle and anxiety implied by the very word "care." It requires carefulness and discipline *not* to violate those closest to us, because none of us is entirely free of the impulse to deny our own availability. How can we not be anxious that our own unfinished business will not cause us inadvertently to harm someone we love? Our impulse may be to put as much space between us and others as possible, or, failing that, to minimize our familiarity with others. But this path is only open to the hermit or the anchorite. The rest of us, even if we live alone, must deal with the challenge of a familiarity that gives us ongoing occasion for violence. Furthermore, if Christian ministry requires us—as I believe it does—to stand in for Jesus in our neighboring of others, then we must seek out occasions to touch one another in ways that heal old wounds. The Jesus of the gospels does not simply refrain from doing violence; nor does he hold back from acting upon others in ways that bring their accessibility to the fore. His healings and exorcisms do more than restore physical and mental health; they reverse the effects of past violence by calling the healed and exorcised to a new life of praise. In other words, Jesus "takes advantage" of these persons' availability in the one way which is not abusive: he makes a claim on their fellowship in the service of God, and in so doing not only heals their souls and bodies but sanctifies them. Are we not also called to use our familiar relationships as occasions for a touch that sanctifies?

Paul suggests as much when he insists that "the unbelieving husband is made holy through his wife, and the unbelieving wife is made holy through her husband" (1 Corinthians 7:14). The wife who treats the husband with the same honor Christ has bestowed on her, and who invites her husband to know Christ as she has known him, will confer on the husband the same holiness Christ has conferred on her, and vice versa. What is this holiness if it is not the capacity to love God and the neighbor without reserve? Such holiness is quite impossible without the assurance that our bodies—and hence our availability—are worth something. However we are related to one another in the bonds of familiarity, we demonstrate this worth to one another by the way we touch one another, both figuratively and literally. Care for each others' bodies—to minister to their sanctification and to avoid wronging each other in them—constitutes one of the chief preoccupations and anxieties of the Christian life.

Finally, care involves the risk of foregoing mutuality without foregoing genuine care for oneself. We often tend to group most of the positive and affirming Christian values under the term "mutuality." For example, we say that there is mutuality in a relationship if both parties consent to it freely, if both exercise equal power, and if there is reciprocal give and take. Thus mutuality has to do with freedom, equality and justice—all necessary conditions for the flourishing of human society. In this sense, mutuality is a biblical value, and any regard for the neighbor that did not include a concern for it would not be worthy of the name. Nevertheless, mutuality does not have much to do with the embrace of nearness. Jesus did not die on the cross in order to reciprocate our love or in the hope that we would return the favor. It is the same with care—which is, after all, the anxiety we take on when we see others as Jesus sees them, and try to exercise the same concern on their behalf as Jesus has exercised on ours. The animating principle of care is not reciprocity.

One of the most striking features of the embrace of nearness is that it is always unilateral. Whether she intends to or not, the neighbor confronts me with a claim on my attention, my witness, and my companionship. The claim is inescapable: the neighbor cannot help but make it, and I cannot avoid receiving it. The neighbor may not wish to make a claim on me and thus may have no intention of returning fellowship, but this has no bearing on the fact that I must respond to the claim one way or the other, and that I am commanded by God to respond with a *yes*. The story of Annie Sullivan and Helen Keller, as it is dramatized in *The Miracle Worker*,[3] both illustrates this principle and celebrates it. Annie, hired by Helen's parents to teach their unruly child and bring her under control, finds in Helen a child who means to make no claim. She wants only to be left alone in the dark and silent world to which she is accustomed. But for her teacher, Helen's whole being is a demand for recognition and release which cannot be rejected, despite all rebuff.

Annie Sullivan's work with Helen is analogous in many ways to Jesus' work with us, not least in its reminder that, like Jesus, the caregiver often finds herself giving herself to someone who cannot and should not know what her giving costs, or who does not even want to be the object of such care. The Summary of the Law ("Love God, and love your neighbor as yourself") places no limit on the extent to which I am to embrace the other as neighbor, save that I am to love him as I love myself. Thus, when it comes to the embrace of nearness, I cannot wait for the other person to go first: I must make the first move. I must embrace the nearness of the other in the hope, but not in the certainty, that my nearness will be received in the same spirit. It is no wonder that for Paul the experience of this embrace is epitomized by anxiety, both for oneself and for one's neighbor. Forcing us to take responsibility for one another, it propels us beyond the usual give-and-take of social life. Its principle is not reciprocity but *kenosis*, self-emptying, and its model is Christ, who "did not regard equality with God as something to be exploited, but emptied himself" (Philippians 2:7).

Thus, if Christian householding is not based on mutuality, neither is it based on equality. Each party takes and is taken, makes an authoritative claim and submits to one. But these do not equal out. Equality in the secular sense finds its ultimate warrant in the notion of the nonavailable self. If *my* self is really autonomous, and *your* self also is completely on its own, then the two of us are equal. We are always on the same footing, because in each of our transactions we are free to opt in or out of any future relation to each other. Our life together is correspondingly artificial—something we have constructed or contracted for together, which we can get out of if we have to, particularly if it threatens the sovereignty of the inner self. But Christian faith knows no such warrant, and it cannot conceive of society in this way. We are always already "in" our connection to one another, and there is no place we can go to "get out" of it. There is such a thing as equality in the Christian sense, but *this* kind of equality finds its warrant in the recognition that the neighbor and I are both created in the image of God. Yet this is a discovery I can make only if I have preceded it by the embrace of the neighbor as neighbor, an act which paradoxically is both the owning of my claim on her and my submission to her claim on me.

Each of us, then, must take responsibility for the care we pledge to one another when we choose to live together in Christ's name. Our care is always unilateral. We can hope that it will be answered with care for *us*, but the fulfillment of this hope must not be a stipulation of the pledge—otherwise it is not care that is being pledged. In the *Book of Common Prayer* the unilateral and unqualified character of the marriage vow is indicated in the directions regarding the taking and loosing of hands. Before making his vow, the man is to face the woman and take her right hand in his. When he has made his vow, "they loose their hands, and the woman, still facing the man, takes his right hand in hers" and makes her vow. Then they loose hands again (BCP 427). What is the point of all this taking and loosing? Surely it is to demonstrate that each vow is unilateral: each party must make it afresh, with no certainty of reciprocation. Of course, there can be no marriage unless *both* the man and the woman take this step. But this is because marriage—like all Christian householding—requires the participation of others who are willing to engage in the adventure of nonreciprocity. I give myself to you utterly not because you are going to give yourself to me, but because you are someone willing to be the person I give myself to. That the vow is unilateral is further borne out by the form of the vow itself: "I take you...." The vow is a particular expression of my claim on the neighbor as one with whom I seek companionship in praising God. If I am taken up on this claim by the other, in such a way that he or she is willing to be "taken" as a companion, then I must do the taking. I must make this claim over and over, without really knowing what the result will be. In so doing I place my identity in his or her hands, as in the eucharist Jesus places himself in the hands of his people.

Notes

1. For a probing study of moral factors leading some Christians *not* to cooperate with Hitler's "Final Solution," see David P. Gushee, *The Righteous Gentiles of the Holocaust: A Christian Interpretation* (Minneapolis: Fortress Press, 1994).

2. *Waiting for God* (New York: Harper and Row, 1951), p. 114.

3. William Gibson, *The Miracle Worker* (New York: Samuel French, Inc., 1956).

Chapter Six

Familiar Disciplines and the Moral Life

Christian householding is both a training ground and a preview of the social life of heaven. As Augustine wrote in *The City of God*, the life of the saints is a social life[1]; Christian householding is one way of taking hold of the life of the saints and making it our own. It is also a discipline, or a nexus of disciplines, by which we learn about holiness and, by God's grace, ready ourselves to receive and live out the new life Christ has won for us.

I have already said that this new life is characterized by *care*, a disposition that reflects the believer's sense of obligation to the partner in householding, together with a healthy fear of the effects of sin—both our own sinfulness and that of others. But for Christians care is not only a feature of householding; it also provides a criterion by which the measure of any particular *kind* of householding can be taken. The presence of care is the litmus test, and an analysis of the disciplines necessary for care should help us develop some fairly clear guidelines for Christians engaged in householding.

Paul's own discussion of marriage in 1 Corinthians 7 illustrates how care can clarify just what a given sort of household should look like if it is to count as Christian. Paul approaches the subject of marriage with remarkably few preconditions. He assumes monogamy, he insists on honoring Jesus' prohibition of divorce, and he matter-of-factly views and endorses marriage as a means of sexual satisfaction. The rest, however, he leaves up in the air. Paul develops a series of positions based not on custom, or social utility, or even direct divine command, but rather upon *care*. Against tremendous pressures to preserve marriage as the norm for everybody, especially women, Paul insists on the Christian's right *not* to marry. This is often interpreted as a rejection of sex, but, as we have seen, that is not what Paul means; he rejects social structures that have nothing to do with the salvation of souls. Paul never suggests that sex between husband and wife stands in the way of salvation. On the contrary, he suggests that the sexual relationship of husband and wife may be a means of sanctifying the unbelieving partner. And it is this possibility of sanctification, and nothing else, which makes marriage pass muster for Paul. It is a form of life together that is life-giving.

But Christian marriage is not the only form of Christian house-holding, if only because marriage and family life is not the only form that human life together takes. The range and variety of Christian households is wide and rich, and in affirming the natural goodness of life together, Christian faith must begin by affirming this diversity. This does not mean that every form of householding is acceptable, because not every living arrangement stands up to the demands of justice and love. For instance, Christians continue to reject polygamy as an acceptable marriage practice. We may acknowledge the economic and social benefits of polygamy in those areas where it has long been the norm and take seriously the hardship involved in asking Christian converts to abandon it, but we still believe that polygamy is not conducive to the sanctification of nearness. If we are honest, furthermore, this kind of reflection will also make us reconsider old positions that may be unnecessarily restrictive. Many Christians are looking again at the moral status of same-sex unions, which have traditionally been rejected as an option for Christians. Here again, the question is one of consonance with the purpose of Christian householding. Are these unions inherently opposed to love of God and neighbor? If they are, then the discussion is over. If they are not, then we must take the trouble to imagine what such a Christian household might look like. In other words, how can a same-sex union serve the ends of Christian care? How well does it train Christians for the wider fellowship of heaven and lead to the sanctification of both partners?

These questions need to be asked of traditional households, too. Christian householding involves working toward certain goals (godly companionship, blessing for the body) and taking certain risks (harming the other, exposing oneself to abuse, turning communion into collusion). Surely the measure of any household is its commitment to achieving these goals and overcoming these risks. But how do we apply this measure? How do we know whether any household is on the right track?

I would like to propose nine disciplines that I think will further the goals of Christian householding and address its risks. The first has to do with our basic commitment to familiarity: the discipline of *bodily fellowship*, by which I mean eating and sleeping together, having sex together (where appropriate), pooling property, and sharing material goods. The second discipline is *exclusivity*. It guards against our temptation to spread ourselves too thin—to take on more familiarity than we can handle and thus short-change the household relationships we already have. The need for exclusivity arises directly from the fact of human sin: if we were not sinners, it would be impossible for us to be spread too thin: we are made, after all, for love, and genuine love can never be used up. But unfortunately we *are* sinners, and our love is never pure. This does not mean that we are not justified in loving some and not others; it does mean that in this life we dare to be familiar with only a few.

By contrast, the third discipline, *accountability to the church*, recalls us to the wider horizon of householding. In God's kingdom there will be no strangers. Christian householding involves a withdrawal into familiarity with a few for the time being, but the danger is that over time we will forget that this withdrawal is a temporary measure whose real purpose is holy engagement with everybody. We may not be able to extend familiarity to everyone, but we must never turn our back on the outsider who is always an omen of the reign of God that is coming and already in our midst. By including accountability to the larger Christian community among the disciplines of Christian householding, we recognize the extent to which the church, especially the local church, can act as a collective "observer" of every household, helping each household to stay on track. The church community can do this because it stands outside the households whose members belong to it. In this sense, it too is an outsider.

These three disciplines—bodily fellowship, exclusivity, and accountability—mark out the basic route that the way of familiarity must follow. Bodily fellowship ensures that actual householding is taking place. Exclusivity and accountability ensure that our householding is properly poised between the demands of familiarity and the demands of universal fellowship. The remaining six disciplines go with exclusivity and accountability in various ways. *Permanence, equality,* and *nonviolence* go hand in hand with exclusivity. They reflect the Christian assumption that we are sinners who can harm and be harmed by those close to us. *Generosity, hospitality,* and *nurture* are part of accountability: each deals with the household's obligation to the stranger. Generosity and hospitality have to do with every household's continuing obligation to those who are outside it, especially to those who need help, while nurture addresses the stranger within the household, whether this be the child who must be reared or the sick family member who requires nursing.

I want to look at these nine disciplines as they function in three more or less "traditional" patterns of Christian householding: Christian marriage, monasticism, and what I call single householding (by which I mean patterns of familiarity that bind a single person to other single people and to families in a more or less common life, either living under one roof or spending large amounts of time together). In the next chapter, we shall consider how these disciplines might play out in same-sex unions.

Bodily fellowship. By definition, all householding (Christian or not) involves bodily fellowship: the sharing of the body's life cheek-by-jowl with others. This fellowship may or may not be desirable or intended, but since Christian householding is always intentional, it implies an affirmation of life together in the body and the constant reaffirmation of life together in Christ's name. The chief mark of this familiarity is willing presence at table, at household prayers, and, in marriage, in the marriage bed. The fellowship that is called for will differ from household to household, and these differences help us to see distinctions between different kinds of households. Thus, according to the traditional formula, marriage is defined by the sharing of "bed and board." This means that husband and wife have sex together and share the common goods of life. By contrast, life in a monastery is single: each monastic sleeps alone, or in a dormitory. Yet this life is not solitary, since, as the most cursory review of any monastic rule will show, daily life revolves around common prayer and common meals. Nuns do not share beds but they do share "board," engaging in an intense communal life that even the closest family can scarcely equal. Obviously, shared meals also play a crucial role in the lives of single people who live alone. Eating with friends often forms the basis for a common life of tremendous resilience, binding together people who do not live together in a pattern of familiarity that borders on householding and shares many features with it. Finally, although common property is not a prerequisite for householding, it may be the sign of a more profound offering of self, of which the turning over of money and other resources is the outward sign. I would like to explore a little further what is entailed in giving oneself over to bodily fellowship, because if we can get this right we will have a purchase on all the other disciplines which cluster around it.

We may begin with the most obvious and pronounced form of fellowship—the physical union of husband and wife in marriage.

In 1 Corinthians Paul understands this union as a turning over of each partner's body to the other:

> The husband should give to his wife her conjugal rights, and likewise the wife to her husband. For the wife does not have authority over her own body, but the husband does; likewise the husband does not have authority over his own body, but the wife does. (7:3-4)

What does Paul mean by this? Does it have any bearing on how Christian householders should approach the discipline of bodily fellowship, even when their householding does not involve sexual relations? First of all, Paul is assuming that the husband's "use" of the wife's body and the wife's "use" of the husband's body in no way alienates the body from its owner. We know this from Paul's discussion of fornication a few verses earlier (6:15f), where Paul assumes that our entire self becomes mixed up with the self of another when we engage in sex: we become "members" of them and they of us. Our bodies cannot be detached from us, as if they were external things to be used or borrowed and given back. We are implicated in what happens to them, because in our bodies we experience our presence in and accessibility to the world. As we saw in chapter three, Paul shows us how this attribute of sex—its capacity to get us mixed up in someone else's self and vice versa—works for good. Husband and wife minister sanctification to each other with their bodies: "The unbelieving husband is made holy through his wife, and the unbelieving wife is made holy through her husband. Otherwise, your children would be unclean, but as it is, they are holy" (1 Corinthians 7:14).

Paul seems to be saying that the bodily fellowship enjoyed in marriage bears fruit in reclaiming a communion that includes sex. What shall we say about householding that doesn't include sex? One might be tempted to say that togetherness without sex has a different communion in mind—one in which our radical availability is not so much redeemed as escaped. On this view, we would rate sexual and nonsexual householding according to our view of nearness. If we were in favor of nearness, we would value marriage more highly than monasticism, but if we were seeking to overcome or transcend our attachment to others, we would put monasticism first. But of course this whole contest is spurious because monasticism does not exclude sex in order to escape nearness, but to explore possibilities for life together that are different from the life of a couple. Then the question becomes: how does the bodily fellowship of the monastery function to reconcile the souls of all its participants to radical availability? How does their eating and praying and laboring lead *them* into paradise?

The familiarity prescribed by the *Rule of St. Benedict*[2] is intense, even relentless. The ancient text leaves no space for privacy—even the brief periods of sleep in the common dormitory are accompanied by the light of a candle shining through the night (Ch. 22). Even if the spiritual path of each can be known fully only by God, nothing in the monastic round permits a brother or sister to think that the path culminates in privacy. One's spiritual journey is everyone's business. If a monk becomes lax in spiritual or physical work—and the *Rule* hardly distinguishes the two—he is to report this to the abbot and make a reparation visible to all (Ch. 46). A brother who makes a mistake in the Office (presumably owing to inattention) must prostrate himself before the community at the conclusion of the service (Ch. 44). To modern ears this sounds like oppressive social control, but that is a misreading of the *Rule*. It would be truer to say that the *Rule* invites a self-giving that goes beyond daily eating and praying together, the pooling of property and sharing of dormitories, and the apparently complete loss of a private life. Sex is prohibited, not because it would encourage familiarity but because, in the context of the monastic life, it would lessen it. Sexual attachments are always private attachments. It is precisely because the *Rule* intends to foster a *group* familiarity that such attachments between individual members of the community are prohibited. Like marriage, the monastic rule invites us to share what is most our own, yet it invites us to share this not with one primary partner, but with a larger (though clearly defined) group. In both forms of householding, the body is given over, in differing though equally unsparing ways, in the hope that the soul will follow.

Note that I say "given over," not "given away." We cannot give over our bodies and our souls in such a way as to lose them, as though they were apples we shared at lunchtime. Our bodies and souls remain our property always. Like our rights to "life, liberty, and the pursuit of happiness," our bodies and souls are inalienable: always our own, in this world and the next. Yet it is possible for something to be my own and for someone else still to have a claim on it. As anyone knows who has enjoyed country walks in England, farmers must not impede access to ancient rights of way even if they pass straight through the farmyard. The land belongs to the farmer, but others have a certain well-defined claim on it. In the case of our souls and bodies, which we cannot get rid of even if we want to, the claim for the Christian is very well-defined: You cannot own my body or my soul, but you have a claim on my companionship as a co-heir with Christ and as a child of God.

Exclusivity. When Christians choose the way of familiarity, they choose it with ardor, taking it up like the cross of glory. The *Book of Common Prayer* gives thanks for marriage by way of giving thanks for the "way of the cross":

> Most gracious God, we give you thanks for your tender love in sending Jesus Christ to come among us, to be born of a human mother, and to make the way of the cross to be the way of life. We thank you, also, for consecrating the union of man and woman in his Name. (BCP 430)

All householding follows the way of the cross, not only because these familiar relationships offer many opportunities for costly witness and sacrifice, but also because the establishment and maintenance of these relationships is done at the expense of any other possible relationships and families. In marriage and monasticism, we agree to turn our backs on other loves and other kinds of householding. Even single householding may require us to draw a line between the people who already count on us for friendship and support, and the many others who may seek it out.

Most obviously, the need for exclusivity goes hand in hand with human weakness and sin, and it is also proportional to the degree of familiarity involved in any given form of household. In marriage, for instance, exclusivity means sexual fidelity. What this really means is that the man and the woman are to honor the nakedness and self-exposure that is their gift to each other, the mode in which they have chosen to walk the way of familiarity together in the name of Christ. To let someone else into this bond of familiarity through adultery contradicts the dictates of care, since we are simply not able to bear this degree of familiarity with more than one person at a time without harming or being harmed.

Exclusivity works itself out differently in monasticism, where sexual familiarity is not an option. As we have seen, the community as a whole is central, as is clear from the priority given to common prayer, common meals, a common routine, common property, and constant presence to one another. Monastic life, at the level of the common life, is intensely familiar. Each monk is accountable to the entire community, and the entire community is accountable to each monk. To be sure, Christian monasticism has usually also honored the path of nonfamiliarity. For instance, the ancient Prologue to the *Rule of St. Benedict* states that for some monastics their life in community will be a preparation for life in the desert. Those who feel a call to the path of nonfamiliarity may well come to the monastery seeking support and a spiritual base for the endeavor of solitude. When they are ready they will be sent on with prayers and good wishes. Nevertheless, the community remains the chief concern, for it is always a sign and a taste of the kingdom of God, which never ceases to be understood as essentially social. For the monk or nun who remains within community, it becomes a lifelong training ground for the boundless familiarity of heaven. For the monk or nun called into the desert or the anchorite's cell, the community becomes an icon for renewed familiarity on the other side of the desert. Therefore the permanent members of such a community, as well as those who travel into the desert, place their spiritual lives in the community's hands. This is why there must be a measure of exclusivity in the monastic life, a means of ensuring that those who are admitted into the monastic household understand the weight of responsibility they bear for the souls of their brothers or sisters. It is also necessary that the internal difficulties and trials of the household not be aired outside the monastery walls—here too exclusivity comes into play. The *Rule* addresses these needs by providing clear guidelines for admission into the household, and for regulating the monks' interactions with the outside world.

What of exclusivity in the single life? Here again it is important to distinguish between absolute singleness—the singleness of a Julian of Norwich—and the more ordinary single life of which most of us have had at least a taste. Many of us pass through "single" periods of our lives as we move from one experience of householding to another; in the meantime, the practice of hospitality, and deep attachment to a circle of friends, make for a pattern of familiarity that might be called "householding in slow motion." For others, there is nothing transitional about this pattern of householding; it is a chosen or at least accepted way of life. In both cases, the regularity of meals shared in various homes, trials weathered together and solitude assuaged, lend these occasions of familiarity a weight over time that turns them into householding. For example, a group of five women in my former parish formed a Bible study and prayer group. When one of them discovered she was terminally ill with cancer, the group carried on and became a genuine household, glued together by prayer and study. After Phyllis died, the other four continued to enjoy a fellowship with one another that could hardly have been more familial even if they had decided to share the same roof. I think also of my own experience as a single seminary student living in the dormitory, or of the small group of single people with whom I regularly spent Christmas and other holidays when I was a curate just out of seminary. In both cases I enjoyed the experience of a common life centered in worship, food, mutual encouragement, and a high degree of self-disclosure. In such circles of friendship—we might consider them open-ended households—exclusivity plays a legitimate role, since where privacy is shared it can also be abused. The gift of familiarity is a gift to be honored and protected, and the inclusion of strangers inside the circle of privacy presents understandable problems if it has not been agreed to by every other member of the group.

Nevertheless, exclusivity can be dangerous because it can so easily be exchanged for exclusiveness, even collusiveness. This happens whenever exclusivity is carried further than is absolutely necessary. Exclusivity has gone too far when it outweighs genuinely universal claims. This is no surprise, since exclusivity is ultimately in the service of universal fellowship and has nothing to fear from it. Even in marriage, we must be careful not to use exclusivity as an excuse for either partner to ignore the legitimate claims of others. We must never let our care for those who are closest to us blind us to the full scope of our ultimate goal, which is familiarity with everyone. Exclusivity has two aspects. It sets up boundaries that protect the household in the name of the wider Christian fellowship, and so teaches us the true meaning of the love that is owed to all.

Exclusivity is virtually the same thing as chastity. In its classical sense, chastity does not mean sexual abstinence so much as the right use of sexuality. For the celibate and the unmarried, this spells abstinence; for the married, however, it means sexual fidelity to the spouse. In some periods chastity has signified godly sexual passion within the bounds of marriage, as well as sexual ardor—even in the midst of a settled abstinence. Edmund Spenser's Elizabethan epic poem, *The Faerie Queene*, devotes the third of its six books to the virtue of chastity. Many modern students of "The Legend of Britomartis, or of Chastitie" are surprised to find that this book is primarily about romantic love, as such love is informed by love of God and profound respect for the sanctity of marriage. Spenser is working off the ancient understanding of chastity as the virtue whereby sexual passion and, more generally, the yearning for familiarity with others, could be subordinated to the love of neighbor without being at the same time repressed. Thus, for Spenser himself, the idea of chastity becomes a way to reassert the dignity and godly power of sexual love in marriage against those who insist that the celibate life is "higher" than the married. Celibacy is one form of chastity, as is marriage.

In our own day we might do well to reconsider the meaning of chastity. If this virtue "orders" sexual desire without trying to pretend it isn't there, and if we approach it as a moral skill in the service of more nearness, not less, then sustained reflection on chastity might provide some fresh perspectives on the vexed issue of sexual misconduct. Unfortunately the guidelines in this area currently being developed by the mainline churches (and their insurance companies) tend to reduce all behaviors to one of two kinds: either sexually-charged exchange, which is prohibited, or purely formal exchange, which is blameless. Obviously, sexually suggestive language and behavior is unacceptable, but I wonder what it will do to the life of the church if we are afraid to express respectful love for one another? What if teachers cannot hold small children on their laps for fear of being accused of child abuse, and clergy cannot touch the sick as they pray for them for fear of being "unprofessional"? Not that most current church guidelines expressly forbid this kind of contact, but their internal logic tends relentlessly in this direction. We need to reclaim a positive doctrine of chastity as the virtue that helps us find the mean between excessive closeness and cold distance, and we need to consider the role of such a virtue in the working out of our sanctification as lovers of God and neighbor. Chastity is central to teaching, pastoring, and therapy, not because it dampens the inclination to nearness but because it purifies it.

Accountability to the larger community. Because householding is dangerous and difficult, households need to be accountable to the household of faith. This larger community is made up of fellow-believers and fellow pilgrims who stand outside our marriages and our monastic communities, perhaps even outside the constellations of friendship and support that constitute the far-flung households of the permanently or temporarily single. These "outsiders" can call us to account for our tendencies to collusion and complicity against God and neighbor, and recall us to tact and forbearance. They can warn us against what looks like abuse or hostility. Such openness to observation and correction does not violate the bounds of privacy anymore than sacramental confession does. Most monastic communities have an official "visitor," often someone who is not a monastic, who can be counted on to speak the truth in love. The national canons of the Episcopal Church similarly call on married persons to bring any family difficulties before their priest while these can still be addressed and resolved,[3] although too often this counsel is not sought (or genuinely offered). Yet the willingness to be observed by a trusted outsider is a sign of genuine care, and therefore an indication that the householders view their householding as a spiritual (and hence ultimately not private) undertaking.

But accountability is not only about staying "on track" and avoiding harmful behavior. When households accept the challenge of accountability, they are also registering their conviction that the household is always the threshold of something larger, the porch of the temple. This is why a family's active membership in a church—and by active I mean *being there*, Sunday by Sunday—is the mark of a family's commitment to a wider community and its desire to be acknowledged as a recognizable spiritual enterprise of the first order. When a household considers itself accountable to the people of God and to the human race, it shows that it has understood the meaning of its exclusivity. As we have remarked before, the discipline of exclusivity (fidelity, chastity, responsible and steady care for one's own household) does not stand opposed to a vision of universal fellowship. It is the only way we can train ourselves for such fellowship, and it is therefore a discipline that we exercise in the name of the whole body of Christ. We withdraw into households in order to ready ourselves for something greater, in order to learn how to touch and to be touched as Christ has touched us. The household is one of the narrow doors through which we may make our way into the fullness of life. To be accountable to the church is therefore to take account of all the others with whom we shall enjoy endless communion in the kingdom—the sisters and brothers whom we have had to exclude for the time being.

But there is more. The household that is accountable to the church also holds the *church* to account, by daily lifting up the social life of the saints as a dimension of the church's eschatological hope. Christian families, and all Christian households, make it impossible for the church to marginalize that hope by turning it into an abstraction. In these varied households children are raised, dying partners are bathed, sexual relations are consummated, stomachs are fed, prayer is offered together in season and out of season. In the face of all these households—indeed *as* all these households—the Christian community discovers whether life together is the church's stumbling block or its cornerstone.

Thus the discipline of accountability has two aspects: it expresses the realism that comes from knowledge of human sinfulness, and it manifests faith in the existence of a vast and enfolding community made righteous by faith. This community, which may turn up in the most unlikely places, is the true church—more or less coextensive with the visible church, but by no means predictably so. This community will rise on the Last Day not only as a cloud of witnesses, but as a host of strangers standing in line for friendship.

Permanence. The need for exclusivity and the need for permanence go hand in hand. The more completely I give myself over to familiarity with someone else, the more reassurance I need. I need to be assured that the relationship I enjoy today will still be in existence tomorrow, and that the companion whose support and fellowship I allow myself to count on now will always stick by me. In Christian marriage the requirement of permanence is unqualified: the intention of both partners must be a "lifelong union." Here again, the sexual relation requires the greatest discipline because it involves the most intense familiarity.

But the monastic tradition also takes this discipline seriously. In the *Rule of St. Benedict,* permanence is called *stability*. Once one enters a certain monastic house, one stays put until one dies or is ordered to a new post. Here it is not, as in marriage, another person, or even a particular group of persons, to whom one promises to stay close. Permanence, like exclusivity, is something owed to the community as a whole, not to the monks or nuns who make up the community at any given time. Members die and new members are admitted, but the monastic house, grounded in obedience to its rule, persists—and it is to this ongoing community that the individual monk or nun vows stability.

What of the single life? Nothing seems more impermanent than this. Not because of any lack of affection and loyalty, but because single householding is so open-ended: there are no hard and fast vows of exclusivity or permanence, and there is no clearly definable standard of bodily fellowship. Very often, singleness is a "home-base" from which the single person moves out, temporarily or permanently, into the way of the anchorite or the wandering pilgrim or into some other form of householding, including monastic life, marriage, and any kind of life where sharing the daily round is a chief feature of the relationship. To this extent, single people can demand no more permanence from each other than they can demand exclusivity.

Nevertheless, just as friendship seems to require some measure of exclusivity, perhaps it requires a measure of stability as well. It is easy to overlook the fact that single people and their friends require physical proximity in order to pursue any kind of life together worthy of the name. E-mail is no substitute for regular times of sharing meals, walking together, sitting quietly in the same room. We do not expect to lose track of friends without warning, or to find that they have moved out of easy physical reach without a good-bye or an explanation. Yet we do not consider their departure in and of itself to be a betrayal—unless, of course, we have had some different form of householding in mind. Is it possible, then, to formulate a discipline of permanence for a circle of friends? We cannot demand that our friends stick around physically, but we can demand that they honor the single householding we have shared, and let us know where they are going and why. In return, we must release them with a blessing.

Equality. The discipline of exclusivity also requires _equality._ I use this word guardedly because of its individualist and legalistic overtones. I do not mean that we are all equal because we are individuals who are equally disconnected and free of obligation. The Christian idea of equality arises from two sources that have nothing to do with individualism. First, we are equal because we are all saved by the blood of Jesus, and are all called to bear our cross and follow him. This is the meaning or weight of Galatians 3:28: "There is no longer Jew or Greek, there is no longer slave or free, there is no longer male and female; for all of you are one in Christ Jesus." These distinctions fade in the face of the fact that we are all called to the same death and the same resurrection: "As many of you as were baptized into Christ have clothed yourselves with Christ" (3:27). Second, Jesus "did not regard equality with God as something to be exploited" (Philippians 2:6). The Word of God took on equality with us by becoming one of us. Thus we are each equal with Jesus. These two notions of equality amount to the same thing. Because Christ died for us, we are worthy of infinite respect; because we are equal with Christ, we are called to give ourselves for the neighbor as he did. Ephesians 5 plays this out from the male perspective: the husband, as part of the church, knows himself to be one for whom Christ died. At the same time he claims his equality with Christ, and offers himself to his wife, thus emulating the work of Christ. We must add that the wife can initiate the same interchange. But as I stressed in chapter five, _this_ equality must not be confused with mutuality. Each may equally serve the other as Christ served us, but the service is always unilateral. We must each own our servanthood and perform our service without the certainty (if not without hope) that it will be reciprocated.

Out of this understanding of equality emerge two requirements for the Christian household: the right of every adult member to witness to Christ and to act on Christ's behalf, and the right to exercise an authority and power within the household equal to each adult's authority and power as a minister in Christ's church. I would like to deal with each of these requirements in turn.

First, every householder has the right to pursue his or her own spiritual path as a disciple of Jesus, as long as this individual pursuit does not betray the basic commitments upon which the household itself is based. Christian householding must assume from the outset that each member is ultimately responsible for following in the footsteps of Christ, but each can and must claim the necessary freedom to follow as he or she is called. This is the biblical basis for the freedom to marry or not to marry, to profess monastic vows or not, to household this way or that or not to household at all, but to wander the face of the earth like the Pilgrim or to be walled up like Julian. But householding and Christian vocation also should not be at odds or make conflicting claims; if they do, then the claims have been misunderstood or are covering up for something else. For instance, Paul says that a spouse ought to be permitted to withdraw from sexual contact for a time for religious reasons (1 Corinthians 7:5). But then it is necessary to come back together, because the sexual relation in marriage is itself integral to the householding, and the householding is also part of the religious path of both partners. Today we tend to be as possessive of our time with one another as of our sexual claims on one another. Conflicts within marriages over vocation, whether to ordained or lay ministries in the church, raise similar issues regarding our freedom to serve God and our obligations toward spouse and family. These can only be resolved when we do the work to ensure that the household path is recognized as a spiritual path of the first order.

This brings us to the second point about equality, namely, that the householding itself be genuinely liberating. Patterns of householding modeled on oppressive political and economic structures cannot serve the ends of Christian care. All too often, the "spiritual" ends of marriage have been touted as an excuse to ignore or condone political and economic inequities embedded in patriarchal marriage and uncritically allowed to pass for Christian marriage. As we have seen, what much of the New Testament literature has to say about marriage goes hand in hand with acquiescence in a socially repressive *status quo*. Women are forbidden speech in church and slaves are commanded to obey their masters—even their nonbelieving masters. Christian householding cannot, however, remain content with such inequities, because the very starting point for this way of life is infinite regard for the other. If Christian householding is about the practice of this regard in the context of familiarity, it forces us to recognize that the other's dignity is at least equal to our own. But to the extent that the gospel supports and endorses life together, Christian life must inevitably produce the Christian household, and this household will include the implementation of equality among its central disciplines. The household structure at which the New Testament aims is a household rooted in the freedom of each householder—no more slaves, no more silent wives. The recognition of this equality has practical consequences for the structuring of power and authority within a household. Where children are concerned, responsible adults exercise authority over them only in order to rear them up to the full measure of their dignity, when they are ready to take responsibility for their own conduct. Where other adults are concerned, the principle of equality must be reflected in structures of shared authority.

From a very early time the monastic tradition has recognized this imperative. Although the Benedictine *Rule* places virtually autocratic power in the hands of the abbot, it goes out of its way not only to remind the abbot he has oversight of monks who are of infinite worth to God, but also to suggest that centralizing authority in the office of abbot is designed to create a space for equality among the other monks. A cynical reading of the *Rule* might conclude that it offers the classic totalitarian formula: total power in one office, equal oppression shared by all. Such a reading might find confirmation in the fact that the abbot stands outside his community in almost every important way. Aside from presiding at the daily office, the abbot does not participate in the common life of the household. He does not sleep or work with his monks, and he has his own table in the refectory. But a careful reading of the *Rule* does not support such cynicism. The abbot is expressly forbidden to tyrannize (Ch. 64). Indeed, he is even forbidden to make important decisions without the counsel of the whole community:

> As often as anything important is to be done in the monastery, the abbot shall call the whole community together and himself explain what the business is. And after having the advice of the brothers, let him ponder it and follow what he judges the wiser course. The reason why we have said all should be called for counsel is that the Lord often reveals what is better to the younger. (Ch. 3)

The abbot symbolizes the authority of Christ, and his chief office is not to control his monks but to enable their growth into the full stature of Christ:

> To be worthy of the task of governing a monastery, the abbot must always remember what his title signifies and act as a superior should. He is believed to hold the place of Christ in the monastery, since he is addressed by the title of Christ.... While helping others to amend by his warnings, he achieves the amendment of his own faults. (Ch. 2)

In the new rule of life of the Society of St. John the Evangelist, a modern Anglican monastic order, the wording is different but the idea is the same:

> The Superior is... the chief pastor of the brethren and has the ultimate responsibility in Christ for the well-being of all.... Al-

though the Superior never acts as confessor within the community and must honor the boundaries of each brother's inner life, he needs to know what is important in the lives of the brothers if he is to serve and cherish them.... The Superior has the freedom to make various decisions about community policy on his own authority. The limits of this freedom are defined by the Statutes and maintained by the collective wisdom of the community. Once a year the community shall hold a discussion in which the Superior's ministry of leadership is reviewed.[4]

In this late twentieth-century document, legitimate power goes hand in hand with care and responsibility for the spiritual health of the community. The superior is given authority, not so that he may lord it over the monks, still less so that he can turn them into children, but in order to support them in the profoundly adult vocation each has taken on. This perspective is not new. The ancient tradition already understands the abbot's authority as a form of spiritual service, not of control. When the Benedictine _Rule_ centralizes power in the hands of the abbot, it is not mimicking the political structure of imperial Rome; rather, it bases itself on an understanding of God's power (as that power was demonstrated on the cross) and in the name of that seeks to undermine—within the monastic community at least—every distinction based on social class or wealth. The rank of the monks is to be determined solely by "the date of their entry, the virtue of their lives, and the decision of the abbot" (Ch. 63). Against the background of the rigidly stratified society of late antiquity, the sixth-century _Rule_ insists on dismissing the gradations of status, so that every monk may discover the reality of equality in the face of God. Moreover, the _Rule_ invites each monk to recall that the abbot is, like them, a child of God who is working out his own salvation in fear and trembling. They are to place their ultimate trust in Christ, not the abbot:

To their fellow monks they show the pure love of brothers; to God, loving fear; to their abbot, unfeigned and humble love.

[But] let them prefer nothing whatever to Christ, and may he
bring us all together to everlasting life. (Ch. 73)

Nonviolence. Everything we have said so far is summed up in the
principle that there must be no violence in a Christian household.
Where violence exists, all prior promises and vows are null and
void, and the victim ought to withdraw from the relationship.

Familiarity means knowing every surface of a person, every
point of weakness and strength, so that the opportunities for
physical and sexual violence are multiplied as well as those for
more subtle erosions and hostilities. It takes great moral skill,
practiced and honed over time, to avoid inflicting these more
subtle violations. Paul's description of love in 1 Corinthians 13 is
a fine catalogue of such moral skills, which might be summed up
in the unbiblical but in our context highly suggestive word *tact*,
from the Latin word meaning "touch." When we cannot help
touching one another, it is important that we learn how to do it
with tact—with delicacy, forbearance, and gentleness. The development of these skills is the essence of householding as a moral
task; through living by all its other disciplines, we are schooled in
touching others as we have been touched by Christ. The certainty
that we will often fail in this endeavor is the true source of that
anxiety and care that Paul wanted to spare his congregation at
Corinth by urging them not to marry.

Generosity, hospitality, and nurture. The remaining three disciplines need little explanation. They reflect the Christian household's accountability and commitment to the church, and hence
to the church's hope of a universal fellowship to be enjoyed by all.

Generosity is often what we mean by stewardship. If our
household life is training for a much larger life, then we must
claim the church as an object of our care and support its work,

which is properly our work as well. One way of making our support concrete is by giving money to support the work we cannot do; another is by giving money directly to those whom the church seeks to help; yet another is by shouldering the work *we* can do, and doing it in the name of the church. Together, these kinds of support bind the Christian household to the church by helping the household take up the church's ministry as its own, by lifting up the church as the larger household of faith and every household's ultimate horizon, and by acknowledging the church's obligation (and therefore the household's obligation) to minister to the outsider and the stranger.

Thus, generosity involves giving to the church. When Christian households perform this service, they not only support the church's work, they also acknowledge an important fact: the church is made up of all the brothers and sisters in Christ from whom we turned aside when we embarked on householding with a familiar few. Stewardship is a sign of our continuing desire to claim this larger community as our own and of our willingness to be claimed by it in turn. Generosity also means giving to the poor—both directly and through the church. By extension, it means welcoming contact with all strangers. Finally, the discipline of generosity involves us not only in sharing our money and our goods, but in carrying out those tasks for which the life of the household makes us especially fit. Note that I am speaking here of the *household's* work, not the work of the individual believer. The work of householding is to embrace nearness by taking on familiarity, and to offer this nearness to God so that it may become holy once again. Attending to this work in faith, with discipline and diligence, accomplishes two things. It witnesses to Jesus, who has embraced nearness with us, and it contributes to the sanctification of the world—what the Jewish mystical tradition calls *tikkun olam,* or the work of repairing the world. Individuals cannot accomplish this witness and this work; it takes two or three gathered together in the Lord's name. Such gatherings come and go, but households may carry on this work of repair for decades, and across many generations.

The disciplines of hospitality are closely related to generosity, since each displays a household's commitment to the outsider. A great deal of attention has been focused on hospitality in recent years.[5] What I would like to emphasize here is the close relationship between hospitality and nurture. By nurture I mean care for the new, the sick, and the dying. This includes the raising of children, looking after aging parents, nursing lovers and friends. These activities and life commitments are akin to hospitality, because the recipient of this kind of care, even if he or she is one's own flesh and blood, is always something of a stranger. Children are strangers by nature, because they come into the picture as if out of nowhere, bringing their unpredictable and sometimes intractable characters and agendas along with them. By contrast, friends and family members whom we thought we knew well become unfamiliar when they are filled with the pain of mental or physical illness, weakened and frustrated by old age, or eclipsed by Alzheimer's or AIDS. It is easier to show hospitality to any number of healthy strangers than to spend years or decades looking after a beloved life partner who has become an enigma and an alien. It may even be easier to open one's home to the homeless than to welcome offspring into one's life and bring them up with patience and kindness. The point here is not to pit nurture against hospitality, but to be aware that a genuine impulse to hospitality may come into its own most truly when we are taxed by the weakness and dependence of those who are most truly our own, or when we are challenged by circumstances to break our households open in order to let newcomers in. I wonder if this is not the most obvious sign of the Christian household in its many forms. Is this healthy and ambitious married couple willing to have a child despite the inconvenience and financial strain? Is this monastic community willing to keep an older brother infantilized by Alzheimer's on the premises, despite the disruption and strain?

The other side of this, of course, is the Christian obligation to accept nurture from others when it is offered. One of the prejudices of our liberal culture is the horror of becoming a "burden" to others. Yet when spouses and partners refuse to give themselves over to the care of their life companions, and when parents shrink from becoming an inconvenience to their adult children, it is likely that the motive is not selflessness but a selfish insistence on remaining "autonomous" at all costs. Most of us are radical individualists at heart, and so cannot bear the thought of being entirely dependent on others. Yet Christian householding is not about autonomy, but connection. When we promise to take care of each other, we also promise to allow others to take care of us.[6] There is no clearer sign of the acceptance of radical availability than the willingness to deliver one's own body over to others, *even before we die.*

Notes

1. *Vita sanctorum socialis est* (*City of God,* Book 19:5, 17).

2. All references are to *The Rule of St. Benedict in English,* ed. Timothy Fry, O.S.B. (Collegeville, Minn.: The Liturgical Press, 1982).

3. Title I. Canon 19. Sec. 1: "When marital unity is imperiled by dissension, it shall be the duty of either or both parties, before contemplating legal action, to lay the matter before a Member of the Clergy, and it shall be the duty of such Member of the Clergy to labor that the parties may be reconciled" (*Constitutions and Canons for the Government of...the Episcopal Church,* 1994), p. 51.

4. *The Rule of the Society of St. John the Evangelist* (Cambridge, Mass.: Cowley Publications, 1997), chapter 13.

5. See especially John Koenig's *New Testament Hospitality: Partnership with Strangers as Promise and Mission* (Philadelphia: Fortress Press, 1985).

6. Thus, the discipline of nurture (and the theology of householding on which it rests) stands in stark opposition to assisted suicide, especially where assisted suicide claims a warrant in the supposed indignity of dependence upon others. Dependence is no indignity to the Christian.

Chapter Seven

Same-Sex Unions

In the last chapter we explored the disciplines needed for life together and how these disciplines are lived out by Christians in marriage, monasticism, and the open-ended householding of single people. Can what we have learned help us to assess and understand less traditional, but perhaps no less Christian, forms of householding? In this chapter we will take up the difficult question of same-sex unions, one generally discussed under the rubric of sexual ethics. Yet the usual debates about human sexuality (what it is, whether it is good or bad, what God intends us to do with it) tend to distract us from the most obvious thing about any relation that calls itself a union, namely, that it is a *household*. Perhaps this is where we should begin. In our explorations so far we have noted a number of moral principles (the disciplines of Christian householding) and sketched out a moral vision (based on the principle of care) that should provide a basis for evaluating same-sex unions as a form of Christian householding. Can such householding be Christian? Approaching the matter this way does not allow us to skirt any of the questions about human sexuality, but it allows us to frame them in a new way. This approach also keeps us from taking our eyes off our chief concern, which is our witness to Christianity as a faith that begins by affirming life together and *then* calls us to make it holy.

That said, we must still begin by talking about sex. The call to bless same-sex unions is forcing the church to be clearer than ever about its attitude toward this dimension of human life. It is one thing to admit that a gay man or a lesbian woman is saddled with the same sexual needs as anyone else and is no less "pulled together" than a heterosexual person attempting to satisfy those needs. It is another to consider those needs to be God-given, without further qualification. Yet that is precisely what is involved in considering gay and lesbian sex as a candidate for holiness. Viewing *any* kind of sexual need as God-given has never come easily for Christians. To the extent that Christians have bought into a negative assessment of sexuality (as if it were something we would not have to deal with if we were not wicked), we have looked to the procreation of children as a way to expiate the shame of our sex. Sex that brought new human life into the world was justified. But a nonprocreative sexuality blows this cover and flushes any lingering contempt for sex out into the open.

I am not saying that the affirmation of gay and lesbian sex forces us to affirm sex without rules. We do not have to choose between a contempt for sex that provides a few escape hatches from shame and an undisciplined sexuality that knows no bounds. To seek a good in sex apart from procreation is not to free sex from moral restraint, but to seek within the sexual act itself something that is morally worthy. The issue is whether a sexual relation, in and of itself, can be viewed as good. If there is nothing inherently evil in sex (in classical moral theological terminology, if the *object* of the sex act is in and of itself good), it follows that we will want to protect and uphold it. For morality is not so much about restriction as it is about celebration: we celebrate goodness by hedging it about with rules, the way we celebrate the existence of children by restricting them and surrounding them with protection. The challenge of homosexuality is not directed against sexual morality, as such. It is directed against a sexual morality that is not thoroughly grounded in the goodness of sex.

Sex should be honored by Christians, not only because it is part of our nature as creatures of God—rejecting our sexual nature is like rejecting our bodies and our emotions—but because it makes plain our connection to one another. Like our need for touch, for conversation, for the sharing of food, joy, and grief, our sexual desires remind us constantly that we are members one of another and cannot flourish without companionship. Sex is easily abused, and our need to use it for selfish reasons can easily get the better of us. But we can also say that our social nature is easily abused and can be harnessed to evil ends; this is what the story of the tower of Babel is all about. We can be savvy about the pitfalls of our sexuality without rejecting it, and, if sex is not evil, it is incumbent upon us not to reject it.

If that is the case, are we not already on the road to the blessing of same-sex unions? If sex is good, and if homosexual sex is capable of sharing in that goodness, should we not accept gay and lesbian sex as we accept heterosexual sex, and then proceed to articulate a sexual morality that applies to everyone, gay or straight?

Let us frame the question as straightforwardly as possible. Is homosexual sex consonant with love of neighbor? If so, may a sexual union between two women or two men be a viable basis for a Christian life together? Although my answer to both questions is yes, I take the counter-arguments seriously, and wish to weigh each of these questions on its own terms. Certainly, we must be very sure of our answer to the first question—whether homosexual sex can exemplify love of neighbor—before we move on to considering the same-sex union as a Christian household. It would be possible to say *yes* to the first question and still have doubts about the second, but if we say *no* the first question, the discussion is already over. We must begin, therefore, by stating what we mean by a relationship that fundamentally rejects nearness.

To reject nearness is to hate the neighbor. Either we love the one who is near, or we use him for our own purposes with no regard to his own good. Any use of another which disregards the other's infinite claim on me as fellow creature and fellow worshiper of God amounts to *ab*-use—the turning aside of anything from its proper function or role. In earlier chapters we noted how easily human beings can abuse one another, whether sexually, physically, or emotionally. This is because we really are meant for contact and connection with one another—like the wonderful toys one finds scattered around the floors of pediatricians' waiting rooms that immediately attract the hands of toddlers because of all the surfaces and shapes they present for grabbing. We are spiritually made for such engagement with one another, but for this reason we can easily be harmed and overwhelmed by one another. This happens whenever we are taken hold of not for companionship but for subordination, selfish pleasure, or sheer destruction.

The gospel calls us to undo this harm, not by retreating from contact with one another but by learning again how to touch one another as Christ has touched us. For the most part this means recovering the true form of our love for one another—reclaiming love from its thralldom to hate. But in some kinds of relationships there is nothing recoverable—the relationship must simply end. Incest between fathers and daughters is a case in point. Where such relationships are concerned, the gospel calls not for redemption but for excision: "If your eye causes you to stumble, tear it out; it is better for you to enter the kingdom of God with one eye than to have two eyes and to be thrown into hell" (Mark 9:47). To ask, therefore, whether a same-sex sexual relation is inherently abusive is to ask whether it is something that has to be torn out rather than redeemed. Is a man's sexual desire for a man, or a woman's sexual desire for a woman, by its nature an attack on the dignity of the one who is desired? For instance, one could think gay and lesbian sex to be wrong, and still shrink from calling it abusive. If so, we might say that such a love, although it did not accord with God's will, could be redeemed.

We can see this distinction being made in a famous passage of Dante's *Divine Comedy*. Dante assumes that homosexual love is "unnatural" because, like most inhabitants of the medieval thought-world, he assumes that sexual intercourse is against nature when it is not directed toward the production of offspring. But he does not go on to call it abusive. In Canto XXVI of *Purgatory* he describes a band of homosexuals making their slow and penitential climb up the mountain of purgatory toward paradise. The salient feature of their ascent is that they proceed round the mountain from right to left rather than from left to right. Their counterclockwise movement indicates that (in Dante's view) their sex was unnatural and hence constitutes a sin against God. But it does not keep them back from the journey to paradise, because their sin was a perversion of love, not an expression of hate.

But some will claim that gay and lesbian sex *is* inherently abusive. Paul's discussion of homosexual sin in Romans is often cited in defense of this position:

> God gave them up in the lusts of their hearts to impurity, to the degrading of their bodies among themselves, because they exchanged the truth about God for a lie and worshiped and served the creature rather than the Creator, who is blessed forever! Amen. For this reason God gave them up to degrading passions. Their women exchanged natural intercourse for un-natural, and in the same way also the men, giving up natural intercourse with women, were consumed with passion for one another. Men committed shameless acts with men and re-ceived in their own persons the due penalty for their error. (1:24-27)

Unquestionably Paul is describing abusive behavior, and singling out homosexual abusive behavior. But such abusiveness is hardly the province of homosexuality alone: heterosexual sex is just as likely to become a field for power plays, annexation, cancellation, and all the rest. Sin lives in all of us, and it is important to remem-ber that in Romans Paul ends up not letting anybody off the hook. By the same token, as Paul is quick to show elsewhere in his writings, sex can become the occasion of sanctification as well as abuse. Why can this not be just as true of homosexuals?

It may be objected that when Paul rejects homosexuality as abusive, he is referring primarily to homosexuality as a revolt against nature. Therefore (so this argument goes), it does not matter how loving or just a homosexual relation may be, since the relation itself is contrary to God's will and therefore stands con-demned from the outset. But this is to shift the ground of the argument by playing fast and free with the meaning of the word _abuse_. Abuse in the strict sense in which I have been using it denotes sexual behavior that commits direct physical or psychological violence against the other. Child molestation is an example of this. But we can also use the word _abuse_ in a more general way. Dante believes, for instance, that homosexual sex is a wrong use of sex, and that therefore those who engage in it get in the way of their own true happiness. But _this_ kind of abuse has nothing to do with neighbor-hatred. This is the point of Dante's treatment of the penitent homosexuals in purgatory: they are expiating a real guilt, but it is not the guilt of hatred, and this makes all the difference between purgatory and hell.

We could imagine using the word _abuse_ to describe a sexual act that is directly harmful to the neighbor yet whose harmfulness is not located specifically in the sexual act itself—for example, marital infidelity. When we pronounce on Paul's meaning in Romans 1, we have to come clean about just what kind of abusiveness we think he has in mind. If we mean that homosexuality is abusive in the strict sense, then we must be able to show that for Paul homosexual sex always constitutes an act of violence. I do not think this can be shown. If, on the other hand, we mean that Paul considers homosexual sex to be unnatural-but-not-violent, then we are saying something different—here the issue is not hatred of neighbor, but error. Here too, I doubt that the charge of unnaturalness will hold up under scrutiny.

How do we really know that a nonabusive homosexuality is possible? On this point the Bible offers us no specific guidance one way or the other. It is fair to say that when the Bible condemns homosexual behavior, it assumes a sexual desire willfully taken up and willfully consummated. Furthermore, the abusive character of such desire is viewed in scripture as the correlative of a premeditated and cool-headed attempt to subvert the authority of God. The desire to have power over against God plays out as the desire to lord it over other human beings, and this "lust for domination" (to borrow Augustine's key phrase) issues in a sexual passion that debases the desirer and the desired alike. But this line of reasoning does not take us as far as we might like to go. We see that the abusiveness that the Bible finds in certain kinds of homosexual behavior is not true of homosexuality as such, but has to do with an abusive intention deliberately expressed in homosexual behavior. This analysis tells us nothing about homosexual behavior in itself, or about homosexual orientation that is neither voluntary nor motivated by a desire to harm others. Since the scriptures give us nothing to go on here, we must fall back on our own experience, guided and shaped (we hope) by the Holy Spirit and by a Christian conscience. This is all Dante had to go on also. His counterclockwise band turns out to include both heroes and friends of the poet, each assigned by Dante to the purgatorial but blessed road to heaven because he *knew* that they were lovers and not haters of their fellow human beings.

In the discussion that follows I shall always begin from the assumption that homosexual sex is *not* inherently abusive. This still does not get us very far toward the blessing of same-sex households. It is not enough to say that homosexual sex is not abusive; if we wish to bless same-sex unions, we must show not only that such unions may be redeemed, but that they also contain enough essential goodness that they can emerge from the (often purgative) process of redemption still looking like a same-sex union. We must be willing to say that a same-sex union, as such, can be the *basis* for a life of sanctifying nearness.

Here we move beyond Dante, who, although he believed that his homosexual friends could be redeemed on the basis of their love, also believed that their sexual relations—even those marked by permanence and fidelity—needed to be put aside. Such relationships could not be a school for holiness because, even if they were not abusive, they would be contrary to the will of God. As far as Dante is concerned, God simply prohibits such sex. But if we are considering the possibility of a Christian household built on the foundation of a same-sex union, then we are considering the possibility of homosexual sex that is blessed by God and does not need to be given up for the sake of spiritual maturity. On this view, Dante is mistaken when he depicts homosexual lovers traveling up the mountain against traffic. If we think of their path as the path we must all follow as we struggle to relearn the love of neighbor, via the way of the anchorite or the way of familiarity, then these couples are simply making their way uphill along the disciple's path shoulder to shoulder with everyone else.

But the tradition stands against us here. By and large (as Dante reminds us), the mainstream Christian traditions have rejected homosexual householding—not so much because they demonize homosexuality (although many do) but because they reject any form of sexual activity that does not include the possibility of procreation. Sex can never be an end in itself for the Christian, it is argued, because taken by itself sex always tends to alienate those who engage in it from God and from each other. Sex itself, of whatever sort, is inherently abusive. On this view, the question of abuse has no bearing on same-sex unions since no sexual relation passes muster in the first place. Heterosexual sex would be all right if it were merely a passionless means of effecting conception; as it is, passion is an unavoidable but strictly accidental feature of the act of procreation—procreation could happen without it. Gay and lesbian sex has no such excuse, and its passion cannot be written off so easily.

I will call this point of view the *restrictive* view of sexuality. It arises from the mistaken but nonetheless powerfully felt conviction that sex alienates us from our own bodies and from one another. It goes without saying that this view prohibits more than gay and lesbian sex: it also prohibits any kind of sex that is not open to the begetting of offspring. The restrictive view was long the warrant for the general Christian prohibition of the use of contraceptives, which is still in effect in the Roman Catholic Church. This assessment of sex as essentially abusive is misguided and unbiblical, but it does take seriously the sanctity of the body, the goodness of the created order, and the inescapable (and ultimately welcome) fact of radical availability. It is not often recognized that authentically Christian distrust of sex does not arise from contempt for the body or flight from the neighbor, but from an attempt to protect the integrity of the body and the dignity of the neighbor against sex's perceived ability to compromise both. Only if we try to understand this distrust will we be in a position to suggest alternative approaches that serve the embrace of nearness and lend support to the argument in favor of the blessing of same-sex unions.

Augustine of Hippo is a key player in the development of the restrictive view, so we will need to look briefly at his contribution. No exploration of the gospel as a call to the embrace of nearness can escape being in debt to Augustine, whose entire theology may be justly viewed as an extended meditation on the command to love the neighbor. Augustine's thought is thoroughly grounded in his affirmation of radical availability, yet he views sexual desire as a sign of our rebellion against it. He interprets sexual passion as the outward manifestation—and punishment—of an inward lust for domination (*libido dominandi*), by which he means the desire to take advantage of the availability of others without having to be available in return. How does he arrive at this conclusion?

Augustine's hostility to sex has nothing to do with its being a passion, for unlike most thinkers of his time, he held our capacity for passion—for feeling and emotion—in high regard. His analysis of the human capacity for feeling (which turns out to be the same thing as our radical availability to God and to one another) cuts against the grain of the pagan philosophical tradition in which he was trained, with its hard and fast distinction between reason and passion. Augustine opposes late antiquity's general contempt for the passions as involuntary disturbances of the soul that threaten and sometimes eclipse reason, and questions the assumption that self-control is the apex of wisdom and spiritual maturity. Far from standing in opposition to the rational will, the passions, whether virtuous or vicious, reveal the will's true inclination. True love of God is itself a kind of passion, and it brings virtuous passions in its wake. The righteous will yields healthy passions, including grief and righteous indignation, and

Augustine is loath to deny that the saints in heaven will experience at least the passions of joy and holy fear. For Augustine, the life of the saints is not only a social life, it is a passionate life.[1]

The exception to Augustine's general account of the passions is his treatment of sexual desire. For Augustine there is no place for sexual desire in heaven, even though his heaven is full of resurrected bodies capable of being ravished with joy in the face of each others' beauty.[2] Here alone, in fact, Augustine's account of the passions reminds us of the classical pagan tradition he is trying to break out of—a tradition which, in treating the passions as something external to the self, lays the philosophical groundwork for radical individualism. He seems to dislike sexual passion because it stands in the way of our control of our bodies, and further, because this lack of control is shameful. Sexual passion is an affront to the dignity of reason.

Yet the real problem for Augustine lies elsewhere. He analyzes sexual desire as the outward sign of an inward desire of the heart, a desire that in itself has nothing to do with sex. This is the lust for domination (*libido dominandi*) I mentioned above. Sexual passion turns out to be the *punishment* inflicted by God on Adam and Eve for their attempt to claim equality with God and to get the better of each other.[3] Augustine theorizes that God's punishment for this sin, spelled out in Genesis 3 (for the man, hard and frustrating toil, for the woman, pain in childbearing and involuntary and humiliating desire for her husband), is a kind of poetic justice. For both the man and the woman punishment is a loss of control and ease (they come to the same thing) in the very areas where God had initially given them dominion and freedom. Adam and Eve reject the limited dominion God gave them in their own sphere because they seek the unlimited dominion of God; consequently they lose even what little they started out with. This may sound harsh to ears troubled by the notion of a punishing God, but it is certainly a fair interpretation of the text of Genesis 3. But then, basing his argument on Romans 1:21-24 ("Though they knew God, they did not honor him as God.... Therefore God gave them up in the lusts of their hearts to impurity, the degrading of their bodies among themselves"), Augustine goes on to suggest that sexual desire emerges as God's crowning punishment for Adam and Eve's disobedience. The idea here is that sexual desire is the same thing as impurity and degradation. Thus sexual desire does not preexist the Fall, but is one of its consequences. It is both the sign and punishment of hatred of God and hatred of neighbor.

It is no wonder that Augustine rejects sexual union as an end in itself, since he views sexual desire as a sign of the Fall. It is also no wonder that procreative capacity and intent become Augustine's litmus test for sex. All sex is illicit unless proven otherwise, but procreation can excuse sex by attaining the goal that sexual union had originally been intended to achieve without desire or passion. However, it is one thing to excuse; it is another to endorse. Augustine never endorses sexual desire, not even in the context of marriage. He argues that the evil of sexual desire is abrogated when a man and a woman bring forth children and care for them, but sexual desire that leads to the procreation of these children remains just as wicked as ever because it is always a sign of our rebellion against radical availability and nearness. Sex is always tinged with the primal sin—hatred of God's sovereignty and of one's availability to the neighbor. If it is directed toward producing offspring, then sex's inherent sinfulness is outweighed by a greater good, like Joseph being sold into slavery by his brothers so that in the end Joseph could save them all from starvation. God may bring good out of evil, but our sin remains. Sex without procreation stands condemned—both in the desiring and in the doing. Homosexual sex, it goes without saying, stands under this condemnation as well.

How does Augustine end up with such conclusions? My own view is that sex bears all the brunt of Augustine's conversion to Christianity without receiving any of the benefits. As a young man, Augustine was a devotee of Manichaeism, one of late antiquity's most harshly body-denying sects. For the Manichees—as for many in this period—sex was a trap, further embroiling those who engaged in it in a world that had been written off as spiritless. Augustine's conversion to Christianity, famously recounted in his

Confessions, was, among other things, a conversion from hatred of the world to love of the world—at least to love of the world as it would be, restored to glory in the age to come. Augustine was converted by the scriptures to the Jewish understanding of God as the good creator of a good though fallen world. Yet sex does not benefit from this conversion. Why? As I read it, Augustine takes the old distaste for sex as the harbinger of a detested nearness, and turns it into a new locus of distaste—this time as the lingering reminder of the old *rejection* of nearness.

Augustine's influence on traditional Christian ethics is incalculable, but his analysis of sexuality is not acceptable. First, it does not fit with human experience. We know how sexual desire can be harnessed to sin, but we also know it quite simply as a feeling or passion that is in itself innocent, though like all feelings it needs to be properly directed and integrated. Second, his analysis does not agree with scripture, for nowhere in the Bible is sexuality or even sexual desire considered a sign of our alienation from God or from one another. Abusive (that is, violent and careless) sex is often denounced as such a sign, as is undisciplined sex (which is indirectly abusive), but never sexual desire as such. From the point of view of scripture, Augustine is also wrong when he identifies sexual passion with lust for domination, for there is nothing in Genesis 3 to suggest that sexual desire emerged as a consequence of Adam and Eve's disobedience, or that it is viewed in any way negatively. The point of Eve's curse is not that she shall have desire for her husband, as if she had never experienced it before, but that now her desire will be for one who lords it over her—one for whom the temptations of power and lordship have become irresistible. The desire is not new, but the circumstances have changed. Augustine's interpretation of Romans 1 is equally dubious: he is reading into it something that is not there. Far from saying that sexual desire as such is a consequence of humanity's fall from grace, Paul claims that sexual desire is one of the things which have been perverted as a result of turning away from God. There is a wide gap between Paul's meaning and Augustine's reading. It is one thing to say that sexual desire is in bondage to sin and needs to be redeemed, but quite another to say that sexual desire is a *consequence* of sin, which shall be done away with when all is redeemed in Christ.

Augustine was the first major theologian to articulate so clearly a doctrine that linked sexuality to the abuse of the neighbor. In so doing, he overturned older negative assumptions about sex—assumptions which, as I have tried to show, linked sex with nearness and rejected it for *that* reason. The result is a mixed blessing. On the one hand, Augustine's account of sex is even more damning than the one it replaces. Sex had been thought of as "irrational," and condemned as such. Now the eclipse of reason that accompanies sexual passion is viewed as God's punishment for a perverse rationality. On the other hand, Augustine's inhumane, almost vicious, reading of human sexual nature is framed within a correspondingly generous concern for the neighbor and an appreciation of the neighbor's ultimate importance for the follower of Christ. To the extent that our discussion has tried to be informed by the same principles, it owes a great debt to Augustine. The challenge, then, is to set the account of sex right without jettisoning Augustine's teaching on love of neighbor. We must reconstruct a sexual ethic which values human sexuality, *even when it is not procreative,* without at the same time surrendering the gospel to the dominant individualism of our day.

This reconstructed sexual ethic is, of course, what we have been aiming at in this discussion of same-sex unions. I have suggested that gay and lesbian sex is not inherently abusive, and is therefore capable of going hand in hand with the embrace of nearness. I have argued, further, that the restrictive view of sex, as laid out by Augustine, contradicts scripture and experience: sexuality is not good because of procreation; it is good all on its own. Therefore, all other things being equal, same-sex unions should be recognized as the basis for viable Christian households. Once this is granted, it is hard to see why faithful sex cannot be godly, even if it is incapable of producing offspring. If sexual passion is not in and of itself a sign of something bad, what need is there to excuse it by appealing to procreation? And if procreation is not necessary to legitimize sex, what is the problem with same-sex unions? Are we not now in a position to endorse their blessing by the church?

Yes and no. There remains one argument against the blessing of same-sex unions that surfaces frequently in the contemporary debate about Christian sexual ethics, one that attempts to recover a sexual ethic affirming the *goodness* of human sexuality. In one form or another, the argument goes something like this:

"It is well and good to insist that homosexual sex is not bad just because it is sex. We also concede that there is nothing essentially abusive about this kind of sex. When a man is sexually attracted to another man, or a woman to another woman, this in no way implies a failure of love of neighbor. When such desire finds satisfaction in the context of a supportive, faithful, and permanent domestic partnership, there is no reason to suppose that it is any less able than its heterosexual counterpart to be the basis for an authentically Christian schooling in charity.

"But [so the argument continues] none of this really touches the central moral issue for Christians. We are called to love the neighbor, and this means especially loving and welcoming the stranger, the newcomer, the outsider. This call is addressed to us in every aspect of our lives, including the sexual, where it comes as the demand to welcome offspring.

"Not that we do not have the duty to procreate responsibly—contraception and family planning certainly have their place. Yet one of the major challenges for Christian ethics today is the secular culture's assumption that parenting is just one of many optional lifestyles that men and women can pursue or reject at will. But the refusal to have children (including difficult or handicapped children) is the refusal to welcome the stranger. When we say *yes* to this refusal in the name of freedom, the ideology of radical individualism wins and the gospel loses. Now, obviously, a same-sex couple cannot procreate, so, although the challenge to welcome the neighbor may meet them in other ways, it cannot meet them in their sex. But isn't this just the problem? If we endorse sexual partnerships that cannot produce children, do we not appear to endorse the refusal of children by couples who can produce them? Is it possible to bless same-sex unions without driving a wedge between sex and the embrace of nearness?"

This argument raises some legitimate concerns. It is vital that we Christians bring the embrace of nearness back to the center of our moral vision, and that we try to let every corner of our lives be judged and renewed in its light. In the case of married sex, this means recovering a solid theology of child-getting and child-rearing that brings out the link between the embrace of nearness in the marriage bed and the embrace of nearness in the birthing room. (We will consider this question more closely in the next chapter). But it is one thing to say that through parenthood heterosexual sex receives its summons to the disciplines of hospitality and nurture, and quite another to argue that since nonprocreative sex does not encounter its summons in this form, it cannot or will not exercise hospitality and nurturing in other ways.

How does this argument slip from one assertion to the other? There is, to begin with, the underlying idea that the sexual relation of the married couple is "completed" somehow by the making of a child. This is notably different from the "restrictive view" of sex, as epitomized by Augustine. Sexual passion is not an unfortunate and unnecessary feature of procreation, but a means of expressing love. Nevertheless, according to this view, sexual passion seeks fulfillment in procreation—sex is meant to be procreative. Homosexual sex cannot compete with heterosexual sex on such terms. But this argument against same-sex unions goes even further, by invoking the idea of the child as the neighbor whose nearness is to be embraced. The result is a remarkable, new, but nevertheless extremely misleading idea, namely, that the making of a child as the object of the sex act and the embrace of nearness as the object of the sex act should be one and the same thing. This assumes that the capacity of the sex act to produce a child and the capacity of the sex act to manifest the embrace of nearness are one and the same. The corollary regarding homosexual sex follows close behind: because it is not procreative, homosexual sex is unable fully to express the embrace of nearness. This does not land us all the way back in Augustine's lap, but it goes a fair distance toward it.

Where does this train of thought go wrong? When it identifies the embrace of nearness in the sexual embrace with the welcome of the child in procreation, this argument fails to notice that sex is an event of nearness _in its own right._ There is no need to look beyond sex to childbirth to see the "completion" of this event. In the sexual act the sexual partner becomes neighbor, completely and irrevocably. Our _yes_ or _no_ to this nearness is manifest primarily in our treatment of our sexual partner, and indirectly in the way we respond to the nearness of others, including the child that may be produced. But it is not the _yes_ to the child that sanctifies the lovemaking of its parents. Their lovemaking is holy if they receive each other as Christ has received them—and if they allow this holiness to infect their lives, they will receive their child in the same way. Just so, a same-sex couple that achieves the embrace of nearness in the name of Christ will be no less sanctified for want of offspring as a result of their lovemaking.

To refuse to assign a different moral value to homosexual and heterosexual sex is not to deny the real differences between them, but it is to say that where we are involved in working out our fundamental attitude toward nearness, the difference is simply irrelevant. If we want to work out what it means to live morally as a noncelibate gay or lesbian person, it is no different from figuring out what it is to live morally as a noncelibate straight person. The task is always to see how the neighbor is to be honored and served, and how everyone's sanctification is to be furthered.

We may turn this around and say that, as far as sexual ethics go, the same moral challenge faces the sexually active gay or lesbian Christian and the sexually active straight Christian. Other factors distinguishing the lives of homosexual people from heterosexual people may make for other moral challenges that _are_ different; for example, the procreative aspect of heterosexual sex presents those couples with a moral terrain some gay or lesbian couples may never traverse. But these challenges and goals will differ to the extent that they move beyond the realm of the sexual. Even then, we may overestimate the differences: married couples may be childless; same-sex couples may become parents through adoption. In any event, homosexual and heterosexual followers of Christ have the same fundamental moral work to do: to love the neighbor with whom they have sex, and to love the neighbor with whom they do not have sex, and to know how differently these two kinds of love play themselves out.

I propose, therefore, that it is not only possible to articulate a sexual ethic that regulates the sexual activity of homosexual persons without prohibiting it, but that this ethic will turn out to be exactly the same for homosexual and for heterosexual persons. I have already suggested that the sexual life of the Christian must be governed by the disciplines of fidelity and lifelong devotion. We can further clarify this by saying that a noncelibate homosexual life lies within the parameters of the Christian moral vision, and that such a life will be marked by faithfulness to one partner for life. As the product of this moral vision, the same-sex union deserves recognition by the churches as an authentic form of Christian householding.

There remains the question of God's will in the matter. If it can be shown that God forbids any homosexual activity—if it is all *porneia* in the strict sense of that word (sex that is by its very nature prohibited, like prohibited food) then of course same-sex householding will not be a legitimate form of life together, however much it may commend itself on other grounds. We must obey God. But for many (including myself) the scriptures do not provide definitive guidance about homosexuality, even though they are unambiguous in their prohibition of any behavior, including sexual behavior, which abuses the neighbor. This is not the place to cover ground that has been traversed and retraversed in the current debate, so a few brief comments will indicate my position.

The passages routinely cited from the Hebrew scriptures to show God's condemnation of all homosexual behavior are Genesis 19 (Sodom and Gomorrah) and Leviticus 18:22 ("[A male] shall not lie with a male as with a woman") and 20:13 ("If a man lies with a male as with a woman, both of them have committed an abomination"). Yet the passage from Genesis is about abusing the stranger, not about homosexuality. The sexual abuse which the men of Sodom undertake to inflict on Lot's three guests happens to be homosexual, but we cannot argue from this to a general condemnation of all homosexual acts—as if to say that any homosexual act repeated the neighbor-hatred of Sodom. As for the prohibitions in Leviticus, these find their warrant in the first *mitzvah* of the Torah (Genesis 1:28: "Be fruitful and multiply"). Given this command, and given God's particular charge to the Hebrew people to become a great people, Leviticus forbids Israelite males from avoiding their duty to produce offspring for the Lord. By the same token, all nonprocreative sexual activity is forbidden—hence the prohibition of homosexual acts.

This prohibition cannot be applied wholesale in the Christian context, although not because the Hebrew scriptures are not binding on the Christian. They *are* binding, but always as received and interpreted in the scriptures of the New Testament. Here is a case in point. We have seen (in earlier chapters) that the New Testament does not take the command to multiply and be fruitful literally: Paul, among other New Testament voices, does not assume that it is the vocation of every follower of Christ to marry and produce children. It might be said, in fact, that Paul urges Christians *not* to marry. Almost from the beginning, Christian advocates for the single life have reinterpreted the command to be fruitful and multiply in a nonliteral sense, extolling virginity as a mode of spiritual fruitfulness. The Christian is called to bring others to Christ, with or without childrearing. We cannot of course argue from this permission not to marry to a scriptural permission to enter into a sexual union with another member of the same sex. But we also cannot argue *against* such permission, on

the basis of Hebrew scriptural texts commanding the literal begetting of literal offspring.

As for the New Testament passages that refer explicitly to
homosexuality (Romans 1:26-27, 1 Corinthians 6:9, and 1 Timothy 1:10), every one of them has to do with patently abusive
behavior. Maddeningly, the passages themselves throw us back
on our own moral judgment: if we can imagine nonabusive homosexual behavior and intention, then we can imagine a homosexuality that does not fall under the Pauline condemnation. The
interpretation of these texts depends largely on our prior experience of and insight into the life together of same-sex partners.
God's condemnation of neighbor-hatred is unmistakable, but this
does not get us off the hook. We must still, with God's help, sort
out where the neighbor-hatred lies.

In all this it is helpful to remember that God's will is never
arbitrary. If the Bible teaches us anything, it is that God's will is
truly our good, and our good is to praise God and to enjoy being
each other's neighbors. If homosexual sex is not inherently abusive—if, like heterosexual sex, it is capable of conveying those who
share it to a level of familiarity that can be the basis for communion in Christ—then I wonder if we are mistaken in thinking God
condemns such sex outright. We cannot enter adequately into this
question here. I will simply say that these considerations lead me
to agree with those who interpret Paul in Romans and 1 Corinthians as condemning homosexual activity when it is abusive, but
not condemning all homosexual acts *as* abusive.

Same-sex unions must fall under the disciplines that should inform all sexual activity, whatever its orientation. As we have
noted, these disciplines include lifelong fidelity and assume sexual abstinence prior to a union or a marriage. I suspect that urging
such disciplines on the church as a whole may prove more controversial than blessing same-sex unions. Some will say that,
while fidelity is certainly a supremely worthy goal, it must not be

attempted without prior experimentation to ensure the right "fit" for a lifetime of sexual restriction. Therefore, these will say, it is morally incumbent on a couple to "see what it is like" before they commit themselves. For some time premarital experimentation has been widely accepted even in church circles—indeed, it is taken for granted. As for "trial" cohabitation before marriage, this is often straightforwardly encouraged. No doubt, if and when same-sex unions are accepted by the culture or in the churches, we will encourage individuals never to consider any sexual relation to be permanent until it is clear that it jives with the orientations of all involved. Others will say that, even if this rule makes sense where the raising of children is involved, it can have no applicability to nonprocreative unions. Still others will urge that no one should be held to permanence at all—it is too hard, and it is unnecessary.

If Christian sexual ethics is to be focused on the sanctification of nearness under the condition of sin, it must center on the holiness of the neighbor-to-neighbor relation in sex, refusing to be distracted by any other consideration until this fundamental concern is dealt with. Paul teaches us that sex is a short-cut to an intense familiarity from which there is no going back. This is exactly what he is talking about when he warns that the most casual sexual encounter binds us to the sexual partner so closely that we can truly talk about our bodies being made one. This familiarity can be a foretaste of the kingdom of God, but, because we are sinners, it can also be destructive and godless. This is the reason for the disciplines by which we regulate our sexual relations.

Loving the neighbor as sexual partner means loving him or her as a fellow householder. There is no such thing as a Christian sexual ethic which is not at the same time a household ethic, since, although there are many ways to be a household that do not involve sexual union, there is no way to have sex with someone without producing a household then and there. For good or ill, we become "family" with anyone we have sex with. I am not claiming that sex produces *viable* households. I am merely saying that it is always the occasion of a familiarity which (unless our hearts are already so hardened as not to notice it) calls out to be honored, protected, and preserved. This is why it is not surprising that sex, if it is not hurtful, usually evokes a desire to create a household to go along with it. The goal of Christian sexual ethics is therefore twofold: to prevent sexual activity from producing a multitude of abortive or competing households and to ensure that the households which sexual activity establishes are safe and holy. What does such a sexual ethic look like?

First, promiscuity is not consonant with a life devoted to the sanctification of nearness. At its worst it exhibits, if not contempt for one's sexual partners (or for oneself), then contempt for nearness itself as the revelation of a real and lasting connection with the other. At its best, it exhibits a naïve or prideful desire to jump the gun on the end of time, an attempt to live out under the condition of sin the realization of a universal communion which is reserved for the saints in light.

Second, infidelity is not consonant with the Christian way, because it clearly does exhibit contempt for neighbor and for nearness alike. This is so not primarily because infidelity involves a breach of contract (that is radical individualism talking), but because it demonstrates a failure to take responsibility for someone who has simply placed himself or herself in one's hands. Even permission from the partner to be unfaithful makes no difference, since it is not in my partner's power to decide how dependent he or she will be on my fidelity. Sex is not a mode of communication that leaves the inner self untouched. The Christian should know this, and should be faithful to the other for the other's sake.

Third, sexual relations should not be entered into unless a lifetime together of spiritual work—a lifelong and exclusive union—is intended. Sex precipitates nearness, and nearness cannot be sanctified unless our actions and, in the end, our disposition toward one another are purged of every pretense to autonomy, every tendency toward collusion, annexation, or domination. I am not saying that Christians should remain in violent and oppressive relationships; I am saying that sexual relationships with built-in escape hatches are not likely to be engaged in the work of sanctification.

The reason for such exclusivity is clear. It is hard to see how sexual relations between more than two persons at a time, or even over time, can further the sanctification of nearness. To be known familiarly is to be exposed to a high risk of shame; to grow used to a certain measure of attention and care is to become more vulnerable to hurt if and when the attention and the care go elsewhere. I do not see how the familiar can really become a path to Christ if it sets people against one another, and this seems to be especially the case where sex is concerned. Competition for attention, jealousy, the playing off one sexual relation against another—these are almost inevitable when familiarity and multiple sexual alliances go hand in hand. No doubt this consideration stands behind the gradual abandonment of polygamy within ancient Judaism, and its rejection by Christianity from the outset. It also speaks against the possibility of a Christian _ménage à trois_, and provides sufficient warrant for the claim that the Christian life—itself one long exercise in the sanctification of nearness—is incompatible with sex outside the bounds of Christian householding.

Notes

1. _The City of God_, trans. Marcus Dods (New York: The Modern Library, 1950), 14:6-10.
2. "I think it can readily be concluded that in the creation of the human body comeliness was more regarded than necessity. In truth, necessity is a transitory thing; and the time is coming when we shall enjoy one another's beauty without any lust—a condition which will specially redound to the praise of the Creator" (_City of God_, 22:24).
3. _City of God_, 14:15-16.

Chapter Eight

The Gift and Heritage of Children

Christian marriage is distinguished from the other forms of Christian householding we have discussed by the fact that it presents the possibility of offspring, applying the disciplines of care to the anticipation, welcome, and rearing of children. This fact alone does not give marriage a higher status, for each form of Christian householding manifests care in response to differing situations and differing challenges; it is usually given to marriage to manifest care in the context of parenthood. But the willingness of Christian couples to embark on parenthood, and the high regard in which the church holds parenthood as a Christian vocation of the first order, demonstrates the essence of Christian love of neighbor as nothing else can. Christians do not have any moral or religious obligation to marry and have children, and so the choice of Christian marriage contains within it a second choice—the choice to become parents, should it be God's will to provide them.

What motivates this choice? If we leave out all the cultural and sociological reasons why a given couple might value parenting, we come down to this: When Christian couples (and the church as a whole) define parenting as a form of love of neighbor, they provide us with proof that by love of neighbor Christians mean the acceptance and affirmation of our radical availability to one another. In endorsing parenthood as a Christian vocation, therefore, the church demonstrates its conviction that *all* Christian living should not only tolerate nearness, but seek it out.

Moreover, when marriage (understood as a way of life that assumes parenting) is claimed as the "mystery" of Christ's love for his church, the Christian affirmation of radical availability is further clarified. Radical availability is not to be viewed as a problem that is inescapable yet temporary, but rather is to be affirmed as a good thing that is permanent—an aspect of eternal life. With this additional clarification we arrive at the full meaning of Christian love of neighbor: the *embrace of nearness*. Here, as always, I mean by the "embrace of nearness" our unqualified *yes* to a permanent relation of availability and communion with the other, where this *yes* is accompanied by the conviction that such availability and communion is and forever will be the true source of our abundance and our joy.

Thus, the church's reverence for marriage provides a moment of priceless clarity about the church's own understanding of love of neighbor—priceless because, as we have seen, it is seldom obvious whether or not love of neighbor includes loving the fact that we belong to the neighbor and are profoundly available to her. We need only recall the error Augustine later repented of, namely, that loving the neighbor means helping her get free of human entanglements so that she can at last enjoy solitude with God. If marriage is the sign of Christ's love for the church, the church's recognition and celebration of marriage as this sign *is itself a sign*: the sign that the church has embraced nearness, and in so doing has returned Christ's love in kind.

I do not mean to suggest that sex is primarily for begetting offspring. As I argued in the last chapter, gay and lesbian sex brings the question of nearness to the fore just as swiftly and powerfully; like heterosexual sex, it can be a means of sanctification. Yet, quite apart from the specific religious significance it has for Christians, marriage is a cultural institution whose chief purpose is to ensure that men and women take responsibility for the children they produce. In almost every culture and every period of history it is the function of marriage to provide a coherent social framework for the procreation and rearing of the next generation. Wherever marriage is taken seriously, its role is primarily to negotiate the impact of children on society's dominant interests. Whatever a society calls its values—wealth, or racial "purity," or certain religious values—that is what it will expect marriage to protect. This is why, in the best societies as in the worst, marriage is a public matter, and why it always involves more than the private business that passes between wife and husband—for example, the alliances of whole families and their fortunes, with the civil authority looking on. All these patterns of marriage register cultural responses to the challenge of parenting the child—whether monogamy or polygamy, arranged marriages or freely-chosen ones, marriages to cement alliances or ensure the orderly transfer of property, marriage as a way of securing social cohesion, or marriage as an exercise in love of neighbor. In some settings marriage is an important economic or dynastic occasion for bringing different families or tribes together. But such alliances are less significant than the fact that the offspring of these marriages learn the necessary moral skills to take their place in the social system. It is the need to offer coherent welcome and initiation to the daughter or son—the need to turn the child from a stranger into a member of the society—that encourages different families and tribes to pledge themselves to cooperation and friendship.

In attempting to meet the challenge of the next generation, marriage also reflects society's attempt to deal with the alien in its midst. The son or daughter is the very paradigm for the stranger who suddenly draws near. As Hannah Arendt once noted (in a determined attempt to be unsentimental), children are interlopers.[1] Furthermore, they are a sign to us adults of our mortality and of our lack of self-sufficiency. We take care of them for awhile, but then we succumb to their care in our old age, and, after we die, we are remembered by them for good or ill. As adults, we often experience children as outsiders. Women may experience them as invaders of their bodies,[2] and even the most loving husbands and wives must resign themselves to the fact that their daughters and sons come between them and erase their privacy. There is no more obvious occasion for the embrace of nearness than the birth of a child, and no more concrete instance of our availability to one another than the ongoing interchange between one generation and the next. No matter how closed a society may be to people it defines as outsiders, it must deal with the outsider in the very offspring its people bring forth.

The front line of the give-and-take of the generations is, of course, the family itself. Exposure to a growing familiarity is built into heterosexual coupling—this is what we often ruefully mean by the word "family." Many of us remember the childhood embarrassment of being openly discussed by adults who seemed to know everything about us. But parents also know what it is to be profoundly known by their own offspring—our weaknesses catalogued, our habits mimicked, our private business casually revealed to anyone who happens to ask. Our children know us backward and forward, whether we intend it or not.

The generation in power must always deal with the fact that the next generation will have the last word, until in turn it too must give way. We may not like the way a given society meets this challenge; for example, we may recoil at the patriarchal notion of marriage as a way for men to accumulate and transfer wealth, using women as pawns along the way. But we must not lose sight of the fact that even here the real issue is not wealth, taken by itself, but wealth as its accumulation and use is affected by the production of children, especially of male children, to whom the wealth must eventually devolve. It may seem odd to suggest that patriarchal models of marriage are built up around fear of the offspring as stranger. Yet if we look dispassionately at the place of children in patriarchy, we see that the child is a dangerously unknown quantity in any society that values the amassing and holding of economic and physical power. Women inevitably share in the precarious status of children. They provide men with male heirs, but they also are closer to those heirs than the patriarch can ever be (witness the Isaac-Rebekah-Jacob triangle)—and they produce female children, too. Because of what adult men in patriarchal societies value, women and children are forever strangers, and they remain unwelcome as long as they cannot be forced to serve the interests of adult men.

What, then, of specifically *Christian* marriage? As Paul and the patristic writers understand it, Christian marriage is not an entirely new departure. Paul clearly assumes that marriage is simply marriage, whether it is Jewish, Christian, or pagan, and the essential elements of marriage are sexual union between a man and a woman with the expectation of begetting and raising sons and daughters. To be sure, Paul lays down rules about how Christians should approach their marriages: they are to do so with the intention of permanence (he invokes Jesus' prohibition of divorce), and they are to do so in the hope of sanctifying each other and their children. But for Paul marriage remains an institution fundamentally oriented to dealing with offspring, and he is interested in restoring a positive and, if I may so put it, eucharistic, meaning to this orientation. The patriarchy that surrounded the early church on every side dealt with the challenge of a new generation as one might negotiate an unavoidable but possibly advantageous risk. Sons could be enlisted as allies in strengthening patriarchal structures, while daughters (if they survived) could be trained to subservience from the day of their birth. Paul sees through all this, I believe, and insists that Christian marriage exists fundamentally as a way to "sanctify" the child, that is, to lift the child up in thanks, as a Jew might lift anything up in thanks in order to hallow it (1 Corinthians 7:14). To offer anything to God in this way is at once to recognize God as its source and to give up all thought of "managing" it, as one might manage a potentially fruitful crisis. Marriage becomes for Paul an exercise in trusting self-abandonment to the presence of the stranger: first Jesus, then one's spouse, then one's daughter or son.

Paul's reflections on marriage in 1 Corinthians are taken up and expanded on in Ephesians 5. We have covered this ground already in chapter four, and it is only necessary to note here that the Ephesians passage is not just about husbands and wives—it is also about families. The passage does not conclude with the final verse of Ephesians 5 ("Each of you, however, should love his wife as himself, and a wife should respect her husband"), but continues on into the next chapter with a series of admonishments to fathers regarding their treatment of their offspring and the new generation regarding their treatment of their parents:

> Children, obey your parents in the Lord, for this is right. "Honor your father and mother"—this is the first commandment with a promise: "so that it may be well with you and you may live long on the earth." And, fathers, do not provoke your children to anger, but bring them up in the discipline and instruction of the Lord. (Ephesians 6:1-4)

On the face of it, this is hardly an unusual sequence; it follows a pattern common in contemporary discussions of household morality, whether Christian, Jewish, or pagan. What is significant here—apart from the anti-patriarchal implication of the whole passage, which is *not* typical of the non-Christian literature of the age—is the fact that the author assumes that marriage and parenthood go together. For the author of Ephesians, marriage is self-giving that issues not only in complete openness and transparency to the other ("the two shall be one flesh"), but also in the complex and often thorny business of family, which is the real culmination of the author's reflections on husbands and wives. In the first section the author appeals to Christian husbands to cast aside their patriarchal privileges and approach their wives as neighbors in whose nearness they rejoice. In the second section, parents are urged to be patient with daughters and sons, who are encouraged to be obedient in turn. We must assume that the same principle that is supposed to shape the husband's attitude to his wife—love of neighbor understood as love of nearness—must also inform the way he treats his children. But can this work the other way? May we read the concerns of the second section back into the concerns of the first? Of course we may. From the very outset of the discussion of marriage, the author of Ephesians has parenthood (in this case fatherhood) as well as spousehood in mind. The whole passage demands of the husband a change of heart that is to transform all of his relationships, beginning with the relationships which are already built into marriage, *and these built-in relationships include the parent-child relation*. In other words, from the very beginning the man is being addressed not only as a husband but also as a father, because in the mind of the author the two roles cannot be separated.

Unless we keep this identification of spousehood with parenthood in view, we will fail to grasp the revolutionary thrust of this passage. We are not dealing merely with a request that husbands treat wives more gently. Such requests are cheap, because they do not require any real change in a system that oppresses women. Ephesians goes much further than this. In requiring a new attitude to the son or daughter as well as the wife, it calls for the husband to take up an entirely new attitude to the stranger—an attitude that requires giving up all pretense to social privilege and all attempts to gain and hold power over others. In the moral imagination of Ephesians, marriage is being alchemized from an institution of social control into one that calls all of its participants, including the offspring who grow up in its embrace, "to live in love, as Christ loved us" (Ephesians 5:2). Thus the passage ends by recalling (adult) children to the fifth commandment: "Honor your father and your mother...that you may live long on the earth." In the context of this passage we recover the original breadth of this commandment, which says to every generation in its prime: "Honor the familiar ones whose place you will take as they decline in strength; as they gave thanks for you and sanctified you when you arrived, a stranger, so give thanks for them and sanctify them as they recede into unfamiliarity." Here we come full circle: the offspring who have been received in the name of nearness and trained up in the skills of a holy familiarity now must apply those skills to their dealings with their own parents. On this view, the succession of generations becomes an opportunity not for keeping things the same (the patriarchal hope) but for starting over again—each encounter with strangeness, whether in birth or in death, a time to place ourselves once again in the hands of the God in whom all things are made new.

All of this is to say that the New Testament renews the meaning of marriage not by uprooting it from its ancient orientation to the next generation, but by demanding that this orientation be governed by welcome rather than fear, by generosity rather than cunning. Christian marriage is not a new *kind* of marriage; it is the old, universal institution restored to its roots in the embrace of nearness. As the *Book of Common Prayer* puts it, marriage is a way of life "established by God in creation" (BCP 423) and it preexists the history of Israel or the foundation of the church. In the passage from Ephesians 5 this restoration is signalled by a quotation from Genesis 2:24: "For this reason a man will leave his father and mother and be joined to his wife, and the two will become one flesh" (Ephesians 5:31). This appeal to a primordial understanding of marriage is anticipated in the gospels, where Jesus forbids divorce by appeal to the same text from Genesis (Matthew 19:4-6; Mark 10:7-9). The church has therefore recognized and honored the institution of marriage wherever it found it, even if it has rejected some of its variations (like polygamy) as inconsistent with Christian care.

By affirming marriage wherever it finds it, as a discipline geared to the integration of the unexpected and the new, the church endorses the institution of marriage as something whose true roots lie in the embrace of our availability to another person. Marriage is a means of *inclusion*, through which human connectedness reasserts itself in each generation. Those who occupy center stage at any given time are constantly reminded by the onset of new players that their freedom to act is rooted in something larger than themselves. Those who are new on the scene need the wisdom of their forbears to learn how to find their way in the world without betraying the web of relations that sustains them.

It is important that we see why the church affirms marriage, even if it cannot always sanction some of the forms that marriage takes. The Christian attitude to marriage in general is a key to understanding what we think is distinctive about *Christian* marriage. To begin with, the church is saying that the perpetuation and historical continuity of the human race is a good thing. Even in its sinfulness, the human race reflects the glory of God, and in Christ it is destined to recover the unity and vitality that was our heritage from the beginning. Marriage plays a crucial role in this recovery by binding parents to their offspring and initiating them into society. The church's affirmation of marriage as an institution that predates the Christian community and exists outside of it is one way the church demonstrates its *yes* to human connection. The gospel does not offer us escape from the human race, but a new reason to rejoice in our membership in it. For it is only as members of this body (the body of Adam and Eve, which is destined to become the body of Christ) that we can hope to enjoy the eternal redemption won for us by Christ.

At the same time, by affirming marriage wherever it finds it the church is taking a critical stance. If marriage is supposed to serve as a means to welcome the stranger, then from a gospel standpoint it must do so honestly, not by subduing the strangeness of the newcomer but by honoring it. If marriage is about making way for the next generation, then it must do so in a manner that reflects the embrace of nearness, not its subversion. Just as it is not enough for a husband to profess respect for his wife without recognizing the authority that she wields in her own right, so it is not enough for parents to welcome their daughters and sons without also intending to let them discover their own vocations, however different these may be from the parents' dreams. Christians affirm marriage wherever they find it, but not the patriarchy by which it is so frequently informed. What is *new* about Christian marriage is not its focus on the succession of generations, but its renewed coherence as a way of life genuinely open to the child as stranger and dedicated to a morality based on connection rather than on the accumulation and maintenance of power.

If a couple's willingness to have children is a clear indication that their sexual union is informed by love of the neighbor, it is equally true that the church's reverence for marriage—and hence for parenthood—proves unequivocally that Christian faith is shaped by a reverence for nearness. It is as if in hallowing marriage the church were to say, "If you want to know what we mean by love of neighbor, look at parenthood." Not that parenthood is the only way to live out love of neighbor—obviously not, since the church has always insisted on the believer's right not to marry, and therefore not to be a parent. Rather, the fact that the church identifies having and raising a new generation with love of neighbor makes it clear that such love means love of a nearness that is boisterous, physical, noisy, messy, and *social*.

Indeed, the church's hallowing of marriage clarifies, as nothing else can, what we understand by the word *love* when it is applied to the work of Jesus. This is the question that has dogged this enquiry from the beginning: is the embrace of nearness a work of mercy which can be dispensed with in the kingdom of God, or is nearness what the reign of God is all about? Is the neighbor something to be used or something to be enjoyed? That is, do we accept our availability to one another for the sake of freedom from one another in the end, or do we begin to let down our defenses gingerly (knowing they are useless anyway), in the hope that encounter with the neighbor may well be a foretaste of heaven? Ephesians' revelation that Christian marriage is a sacramental sign of Christ's love for the church provides a definitive answer to this question. When we call Jesus neighbor, brother, and friend, we are claiming that Jesus wants to be radically available to us, and we are professing a desire to be radically available to him. This claim and this desire constitute the definitive center of the Christian life.

In lifting up lifelong procreative marriage as the emblem of Christ's love for us, the church identifies Jesus' self-giving with the affirmation of nearness entailed in all willing parenthood, and so makes it clear that the believer's relation with Jesus is not an escape from the body or the world, but just the opposite. If the embrace of nearness is like Jesus' embrace of us, then that embrace cannot be a mere bridge to something else: *it must itself be the goal.* The nearness of Jesus is an end in itself: it is our salvation, joy, and fulfillment. Once we have come into contact with the love of Jesus, we know that it is possible to enjoy God and the neighbor at the same time; in Jesus we are offered both at once. And if nearness to our human brother Jesus is our true good, so is nearness to every other human being. The link Ephesians makes between marriage as the welcome of the child and Jesus' love for each of us is like the "x" on a map showing where the secret treasure lies. The treasure is not something we can enjoy in private; it only exists in the company of the other: poor, homosexual, female, *in utero*, non-Christian, ethnically different, differently abled. But this treasure is worth selling everything—losing all one's pretended self-sufficiency and purity—to gain.

All other kinds of householding are also liable to misinterpretation in this regard. Apart from marriage, the forms of Christian householding are unambiguously anti-patriarchal, but they are not unambiguously anti-individualist. For instance, I can love my friend because, as Aristotle said, he is "another self," a mirror in which I see myself at my best. But it is quite possible to conclude from Aristotle that my friend is of use to me only as long as I am striving to achieve my personal best—even the noblest friendship must inevitably be outgrown, when the goal that gave it meaning has been reached. On this view, the friend is like a pacesetter, someone who will run the race with me. Once I win the race, even if it is a noncompetitive race to achieve moral excellence, I no longer need him. Most people I know do not regard their friends in this way, and most friendships do not look like this—certainly, few Christians would want to characterize their friendships in this way. Yet there is nothing about the outward form of friendship—the space each must afford the other, the benefit each undeniably reaps from the other, the equality and independence that each must maintain—that argues against Aristotle's view of friendship.

We can observe the same ambiguity in the idea of the monastic life. I have suggested that Christian monasticism is essentially a schooling in intense familiarity with a number of people, with a view to readying the soul for even more familiarity in heaven. But if we are looking in from the outside, this is not obvious. Monasticism can be and has been interpreted as group support for solitude with God. In a way, the various rules of life that have shaped Christian monasticism and the great works on virginity and the monastic life that occupy such an important place in the patristic literature are all informed by their authors' desire to clarify, both for the monastics and for the rest of us, that being a monk or nun is *not* about fleeing nearness.[3]

Taken by itself, sexual union is no less ambiguous. The fruits of a long, charitable, and faithful relationship are not ambiguous, but the mere fact of long-term sexual engagement with another person of either sex does not itself express commitment to nearness. The mere *form* of committed sexual partnership says nothing one way or the other about the relation of this partnership to those who stand outside it. Romantic literature is full of nonbelieving lovers who care about nothing and no one beyond their own love for one another.

Compared to the outward form of marriage, the outward forms of friendship, monasticism, and sexual union are surprisingly opaque when it comes to the subject of nearness. There is nothing about the idea of a celibate life in community which, all by itself, will indicate to the religious novice that she is embarking on a way of life inviting more nearness, not less. There is nothing in a close friendship that could prevent us from assuming that the relationship is ultimately utilitarian. Similarly, the more ardent the love affair, the more difficult it is to tell from the outside where charity ends and idolatry begins.

This is not to suggest, of course, that friendship, the monastic life, and sexual love are not fit vehicles for the Christian life. Quite the opposite. The embrace of the neighbor can flourish gloriously in these contexts. But the church's endorsement of marriage clarifies precisely what it is that we are meant to applaud when we lift up these forms of Christian householding. Parental anxiety is the type of all Christian care. If we are not sure what Christian care means, we can simply think about being a parent and the notion of care will come immediately into focus. Here there is certainly no reciprocity, no mutuality: the child must be nurtured and enabled to flourish not for the sake of the parents, but for his or her own sake. By this criterion any Christian household, whether or not it is grounded in marriage, can assess itself with regard to love of neighbor. All life together—whether it be with one's partner, spouse, brother or sister monastic, or friend—is to be understood this way: as we respect the child as a stranger in our midst, so we must accept the otherness of lover, spouse, and fellow traveler. If members of a household feel a genuine obligation toward their fellow householders, one that goes beyond mere reciprocity, then genuine love of neighbor is present. This sense of obligation is the source of the anxiety or care that Paul associates with any true love of neighbor—whether that neighbor be Jesus (in which case we are anxious to carry out his will in the world), or our spouses, partners, friends, and fellow monastics (in which case we are anxious to ensure their physical and spiritual health). If this care is absent, love of neighbor is probably absent, too.

Yet—and I cannot overemphasize this point—marriage has no monopoly on the sanctification of nearness. Christians who have a vocation to marriage serve the church by perpetuating a way of life with incalculable symbolic value for the Christian community as a whole. Beyond that, they are simply doing the best they can, along with everyone else, to love their fellow householders in Christ's name. Love and fidelity, not progeny, are the mark of a godly sexual relationship. Procreation has no greater value than sticking by the partner who is dying of AIDS or breast cancer, or choosing celibacy in order to minister more effectively to more people. Rather, the identification of parenthood with love of neighbor is the hermeneutical key that unlocks the ultimate meaning of any life together that is lived out in Christ's name. Wherever all insistence on mutuality and autonomy has been cast aside, there the Christian household can be found. All households in which such love is exercised can claim the church's theology of marriage as a warrant for their own right to be taken seriously.

All this is well and good, as far as it goes. Who would not wish to be able, on Christian principles, to hold a high theology of marriage that at the same time provided a solid theological basis for honoring a wide range of Christian households, including same-sex unions? But do we gain such a theology at the expense of reproductive choice? If we insist that the procreativity of marriage provides a warrant for all kinds of Christian households, what are the practical implications for married couples? Many married couples do not choose to become parents. If Christian same-sex couples eventually enjoy the blessing of the church, even though their sexual intercourse cannot produce children, why should Christian heterosexual couples alone bear the burden of parenthood—especially when contraception is so easily available? Why should *they* be a sign of the embrace of nearness by seeking to become parents, when no one else has to?

The only honest answer is that the embrace of nearness always finds new occasions for its exercise. Procreation may not be the end of sex, but for heterosexual couples it is very likely—apart from cases of infertility—to be a consequence of sex, unless measures are taken to prevent conception. What does it mean for a Christian couple to decide never to allow conception to take place? Leaving aside the difficult questions connected with hereditary disease or fetal abnormalities, we may well ask whether a refusal to be parents—whether for the sake of lifestyle or because one is simply afraid—is consonant with the embrace of nearness. Does not the same criterion that excuses gay men and lesbian women from parenthood (without precluding it) lay on straight couples the imperative to take parenthood on if possible? I think it does. The refusal to parent children calls into question the nature of the sexual union because it is such a blatant rejection of the neighbor—the neighbor here being a child.

Adult ambivalence about the child is understandable, as is any child's ambivalence about parents. It is understandable because our dislike of availability is understandable and universal. But for the Christian such ambivalence is a sin to be overcome. We may each have our own private struggles with a fear of or distaste for nearness, but our convictions, if they are informed by faith in Jesus, must stand unequivocally on the side of love of neighbor as the ultimate value. This is why it is so important that the church affirm parenthood. It is understandable that the church should for pastoral reasons stand by married couples who cannot on good faith enter into parenthood (because of genetics, for example). But the church's willingness to consider procreation as a separate issue from marriage casts its theology of marriage into doubt by raising the question whether marriage is, after all, rooted in the embrace of nearness. Heterosexual union is, for Christians, a way to embrace the neighbor and to sanctify nearness in the name of Jesus, with a view to the neighboring of others along the way. Christians do this knowing that in the end they will enjoy communion—ecstatic nearness—with everyone in the kingdom of God. If such a union is likely in the normal course of things to lead to conception and childbirth, and if the advent of the child is an obvious occasion for a couple appropriately to extend their love for each other to a third person, what does it mean if the Christian heterosexual couple decides ahead of time that they will not permit any child to be born?

An analogy might clarify what I am saying here. If a Christian man falls in love with another man, and consecrates his sexual union with him in the name of Christ, he is witnessing to the fact that this union is not grounded in selfishness—either in his own private ends or in the private ends of the partnership. It is based rather in a desire to begin to learn how to live with others the life of fellowship that has been experienced with Jesus, starting with this life partner. So we would be surprised if other opportunities for fellowship were passed by, especially if this opportunity grew directly out of the life of the household and did not compromise its integrity. Suppose the partner's small child by a previous marriage becomes motherless. If the Christian partner is unwilling to take in the child because of the inconvenience and change of lifestyle this would entail, then we would question the original intent in entering into the sexual union. Not that the man's love for his partner was not genuine, but the frame around it would turn out to be smaller than we had thought. His love might well be faithful in the romantic sense, but its ultimate intentions would be questionable from the Christian point of view, because, for all its faithfulness, it would be rooted in something less than the love of nearness. The point is not merely that sexual love should come clean by accepting responsibility for children. The obligation to welcome children has nothing to do with sexual ethics, *per se;* we would expect the same kind of responsibility from a single person or a monastic community.

Someone will say that our care for a real daughter or son who already exists is different from our willingness to bring into the world a child who does not yet exist, and who may never exist. But this objection does not get to the heart of the matter. The problem lies in the decisions we make to limit our openness to the neighbor. Drawing limits is necessary—that is what the discipline of exclusivity is all about. But exclusivity in this sense is not the same thing as exclusion. I must exercise exclusivity when it comes to sex, because to break the bond of fidelity with my spouse would be to launch a frontal attack on the integrity of my marriage. But this exclusivity certainly does not prohibit me from being deeply attached to my young daughters, nor should it keep me from concerning myself materially with the needs and concerns of the homeless people who sleep within yards of my wife's and my bedroom window. Of course, there are always limits to what we can do; but there is usually someone who has an immediate claim upon us, and our response to this immediate claim is a measure of our seriousness about embracing nearness. Consider again the case of the man whose child had lost his mother. What if the man's partner were dying? In that case we might not expect him also to take on guardianship of the child. Rather, we would expect him to leave no stone unturned to find another home for the child, so that he could devote himself wholeheartedly to taking care of his sick partner. In other words, the claim of the sick partner is more immediate than the claim of the child. But the rule of immediacy does not release us from the obligation to open our lives to the stranger, whether the stranger be a child, or a partner who has become dependent (and therefore a stranger) owing to sickness. If a married couple has decided never to have children because it does not accord with their own plans for success or pleasure, they are open to the suspicion that in other areas of their lives they are also closed to the claim of the stranger. Most heterosexual couples must go out of their way to prevent the conceiving of children (even though infertility seems to be more common in my generation). Thus, it is not a question of rejecting this child or that, but of deciding to forego one whole area of love of neighbor—love of offspring. Such decisions are not consistent with the spirit of Christian householding which, when all is said and done, is adventuresome and freewheeling. Within our limited capacities we must turn ourselves over to the neighbor and then be willing to take what comes, without second-guessing the outcome.

This is not an argument against birth control. We *do* have limited capacities for raising children properly, and the earth yields limited resources to sustain its population of human beings. In the light of such considerations it is not a betrayal of the moral adventure to take measures to regulate and limit the conception of offspring. But we can accept the wisdom of birth control without denying the essential relation between marriage and procreation. It is not how many children we have that counts; it is whether we are willing to have any at all. There are, I think, good reasons for choosing not to have children: illness, age, mental instability. Only the couples involved can judge whether their reasons are morally compelling, and their judgment must be respected on the assumption that it is informed by conscience. Nevertheless—and this is my main point—Christian conscience needs to be sure that the decision not to be a parent does not arise from a rejection of nearness.

An argument in favor of parenting is not an argument in favor of patriarchy. Because reproductive choice is so closely linked with the liberation of women, it is easy to assume that patriarchy and having lots of children go together. But the connection between the two ideas is accidental. For example, a patriarchal system could be imagined in which easy contraception and few children would go hand in hand with oppressive conditions for both women and children. When I talk about openness to children as a sign of the embrace of nearness, I am talking about a disposition that is fundamentally at odds with patriarchy because it rejects any notion of the son or daughter (and therefore also of the mother) as an extension of the father. It is the offspring as stranger (not as extension) who is welcomed.

Do the presuppositions of Christian householding provide a fresh starting-point for the vexed issue of abortion? If the child is *always* to be viewed as a stranger, and if the claim of the stranger is part and parcel of Christian householding, then the unborn child has a claim that the Christian is hard put to deny. This claim is particularly strong when it can be addressed to *both* parents, since every sexual relation between a man and a woman is implicitly the establishment of a household. If the parents are living together and they produce a child, the disciplines of householding demand that they should allow the fetus to come to term and should welcome the child into their midst. This is far less clearly the case when the mother has been abandoned, and still less so when she is the victim of rape. Yet even here the Christian moral vision, inasmuch as it is shaped by the embrace of nearness, cannot discount the moral worth of bringing the unwanted child to birth. This is not to deny the woman's right to make her own decision in this matter, but simply to suggest that, for the Christian woman, the claim of the unborn child may well outweigh her need to rid herself in every possible way of the consequence of her mistreatment and violation.

Of course, many married people who want to have children are unable to do so. But their desire for children, even in a marriage where children are an impossibility (either biologically or by adoption) is evidence in itself that the marriage is grounded in the embrace of nearness and seeks to bear fruit in service to the neighbor. Such couples will find this fruition one way or another—if not by adopting children, then in some other way, as, for example, couples who are "uncle" and "aunt" to many children who are not related to them biologically. At any rate, where it is both physically possible and morally responsible, procreation is for Christians not merely a reason to be married; parenthood is a vocation to be followed.

Our discussion of marriage has implications for the way we think about the conjugal family that emerges from a heterosexual couple's willingness to rear children. If the church's affirmation of marriage (including procreation) is a key to interpreting the church's embrace of nearness, then surely the family is part of what the church is affirming when it affirms marriage. Moreover, as a marriage's *yes* to nearness unfolds through time, the family shares in the revelatory power of Christian marriage. It too is a sacramental sign not only of Christ's love for the church but of the church's embrace of nearness. However, just as Christian marriage is no holier than any other form of Christian householding, the families to which it gives rise are no holier than any other kinds of households in which children are being raised, or any better equipped to live up to the love of Jesus. The conjugal family's importance for Christians lies in the fact that in this way of life marriage fulfills itself as the unequivocal sign of the love of neighbor commanded by Jesus.

It is virtually impossible, however, to assert the value of the conjugal family without being misunderstood. We live in a culture where strong endorsements of marriage and family often accompany nostalgia for patriarchal traditions and provide encouragement for open or covert attacks on gay and lesbian persons, as well as on members of religious orders. The rhetoric of "family values" is now almost synonymous with "patriarchal values," and, it goes without saying, is aimed against gay men, lesbian women, and women generally. Marital fidelity, sexual abstinence before marriage, the willingness to be parents in the first place, responsibility for one's own daughters and sons and a concern for their proper initiation into social life—all of these duties follow from Christian care. But all too often these duties are linked to political values that have nothing to do with the embrace of nearness, and everything to do with classic patriarchy. These "values" include insistence on the father's role as head of the family, prohibitions against women assuming leadership positions outside the home, defense of a father's right to use corporal punishment on his offspring (though few would dare to say he could use it on the offspring's mother), and encouraging mothers (but not fathers) to avoid work outside the home.

Christian proponents of these values can easily cite scriptural passages that will support their views, but to do this they must ignore the ambivalence which in the final analysis marks the New Testament attitude to patriarchy. As we saw in chapter four, the New Testament texts reveal the traces of an anti-patriarchal streak within the early church, and these traces function even now to create fruitful tensions in the most patriarchal of New Testament passages. Since we are perhaps in a better position than our ancestors to notice these tensions—for all its sexism our age is, we hope, less *unconsciously* patriarchal—the refusal of Christians to take them into account suggests more than an unthinking bias. It suggests that a conscious choice is being made to put women down and keep the neighbor at bay. But such choices have little to do with Jesus, who has embraced each of us as if we were a child.

Notes

1. *The Human Condition* (Chicago: The University of Chicago Press, 1958), p. 242.
2. The notion of the fetus as invader and of the mother as unwilling host figures centrally in the debate over abortion rights. In conjunction with a moral vision grounded in autonomy, it provides a powerful warrant for abortion. But such arguments are not consonant with the embrace of nearness. Does autonomy outweigh the claim of the stranger? It is one thing, of course, to compel unwilling women to bear children; it is quite another to ask whether, as believing Christians, we can employ the arguments of radical individualism to legitimize the termination of pregnancy.

3. Augustine's treatise *On Virginity* is exemplary in this regard. The entire work is intended to remind monastics that their vocation is not supposed to lift them above the world but rather to immerse them in it as witnesses of Christ. Christ came to minister to all, so those who have taken the vow of celibacy must also minister to all. Augustine drives his argument home with a reference to the virgins of Revelation 14:4, who "follow the Lamb wherever he goes." The lamb, of course, is Jesus, and the path he follows is guided by the embrace of nearness with every human being. So also for the monastic: to follow Jesus is not to escape the world, but to enter more deeply into it, that it may be sanctified: "Himself lifteth up such as follow in lowly wise, Who thought it not a trouble to come down unto such as lay low" (*On Virginity*, trans. C. L. Cornish in *Nicene and Post-Nicene Fathers*, ed. Philip Schaff [Grand Rapids: Eerdmans Publishing Co., 1980/1887], Vol. 3, p. 436).

Epilogue

Householding is a way of sanctification. It can heal us of our inattention to one another, and teach us how to enjoy our nearness to one another in Christ. If this twofold purpose is served, it hardly matters what form the householding takes. There is no healing in any form of householding that does not take our sinfulness and our need for discipline seriously, and there is no joy in any householding that does not ally itself with the claim of every neighbor and with all who place their hope in a universal reign of peace. Christian marriage and Christian monasticism are justified by this discipline and this hope; apart from this justification, neither marriage nor monasticism has any claim upon us. If other ways of construing the Christian household can demonstrate a similar discipline and a similar hope, they too should be taken seriously and honored. This is the basis on which I have endorsed the blessing of same-sex unions.

But the gate is narrow. Redeemed familiarity is arduous, not cheap. For the Christian, holy familiarity begins with Jesus and works itself out from there, sometimes with fear and trembling, sometimes in joy and confidence. Promiscuous relations do not make for schooling in familiarity. This is the tension at the heart of Christian (and I suppose of any truly religious) householding: we must distance ourselves from some in order to learn what it means to be a neighbor to all.

In relation to this tension the church has a tricky and difficult path to tread. The church (even though she is divided) is a society meant to be a foretaste of our communion with one another in heaven. We may not often achieve this threshold of communion, but this achievement reveals what we really *are*, insofar as we manage to be God's church at all. So the common life and worship of the church is a constant reminder of what Christian household-ing is all about. Christian householding is preparing us for holy familiarity with everyone by providing an opportunity for concrete familiarity with just a few people; the church, as a sign of my bond with all followers of Jesus, is a constant reminder that in heaven my experience of familiarity is going to transcend my present household ties. Thus, the church challenges all her households not to make idols of themselves, but to remember their ultimate loyalty to Jesus and to all for whom he died.

But the household presents a challenge for the church as well. As the church, we may be tempted to a kind of spurious house-holding, pretending to a familiarity with one another that is un-real because it has not been forged in the crucible of day-to-day life together. This is particularly a temptation for the modern North American parish. The desire—itself commendable—to provide people with a parish "home" may all too easily become the occasion to envision the congregation as if it were a household or "family." The challenge is to let the sanctuary be both a space around us and a space between us, where we can give thanks for the fellowship that is already ours in hope, without trying to turn the church into an imitation of the household, still less a substi-tute for it.

Practically speaking, this means less emphasis on the parish as a "family" and more emphasis on the parish as a public meeting place for all kinds of households, including single households. We must recognize that the parish is risky—for families as well as single people—for in the parish private familiarities become pub-lic business as we invite accountability to the body of Christ. Great tact is required here, because the integrity of the household (which has heretofore been secured through some measure of privacy) is now exposed to the possibility of assimilation into the life of the parish. The parish must counteract this danger by striving to be more than a local club. When the parish becomes the sacrament of universal fellowship, the place where infinite regard *even for the stranger* is lifted up as the goal of the Christian life, then and only then can the parish become a window onto that heavenly city which gives Christian householding its direction and its point.

In this book we have not begun to explore how the church (especially the local parish) might better honor, challenge, and support the households in its midst. That is a task for another day. But perhaps these questions are best asked and answered in the local context. The crucial thing is for all of us, individually and corporately, to determine just where we stand with respect to life together. Do we view it as joy or sorrow? Do we want Jesus to lead us into nearness or to deliver us from it?

A student at General Seminary told me a story which illustrates this choice dramatically. For some years she served as deacon in an Episcopal drop-in center for the homeless called St. Lawrence's Chapel.[1] When the center was still in its early days (a large, hot, corrugated metal building with a few showers, a kitchen, and a makeshift altar at one end), the clergy on the staff decided to conduct a Maundy Thursday service that included the traditional foot-washing. Twelve clients volunteered to have their feet washed by the clergy. Thanks to the facilities at the center, they were able to wash their own feet before the official rite. All but one. This man arrived just before the service with his leg in a cast, upset and embarrassed because he could not reach his feet (which were filthy) to "get them decent." Just as the scene was about to issue into laughter at this man's expense, one of the homeless volunteers simply grabbed the towel and the bowl that stood ready for the ritual washing, filled the bowl with water, and washed the man's feet.

This event was a turning point for the center. The Maundy Thursday service has never been the same: participants are as likely to wash as to be washed, whether or not they are homeless, clergy or lay, clients or staff—and there is no "pre-washing." Most importantly, St. Lawrence's Chapel has become less a safety zone homeless people drift in and out of, and more a community of care for homeless and center staff alike.

The transformation of St. Lawrence's Chapel happened because a homeless man was moved to regard a neighbor's exposure to judgment as an occasion of communion rather than of shame. What this man did for one community, Jesus did for us all. His embrace of nearness (which we experience as grace) is the only plausible basis any Christian has for taking community seriously, not only as a moral imperative but as the key to all our happiness. May God help us to see that Christ brings nearness and nothing else—there is no grace that does not call us to a crowded but abundant feast.

Notes
1. I am indebted to the Rev. Lynn Ramshaw for this story. St. Lawrence's Chapel is in Pompono Beach, Florida.